Chen T'ai Chi
Traditional Instructions from the Chen Village
Volume 2

An Anthology of Articles from the *Journal of Asian Martial Arts*
Edited by Michael A. DeMarco, M.A.

Disclaimer
Please note that the authors and publisher of this book are not responsible in any manner whatsoever for any injury that may result from practicing the techniques and/or following the instructions given within. Since the physical activities described herein may be too strenuous in nature for some readers to engage in safely, it is essential that a physician be consulted prior to training.

All Rights Reserved
No part of this publication, including illustrations, may be reproduced or utilized in any form or by any means, electronic or mechanical, including photocopying, recording, or by any information storage and retrieval system (beyond that copying permitted by sections 107 and 108 of the US Copyright Law and except by reviewers for the public press), without written permission from Via Media Publishing Company.

Warning: Any unauthorized act in relation to a copyright work may result in both a civil claim for damages and criminal prosecution.

Copyright © 2015 by
Via Media Publishing Company
941 Calle Mejia #822
Santa Fe, NM 87501 USA
E-mail: md@goviamedia.com

All articles in this anthology were originally published in the *Journal of Asian Martial Arts*.
Listed according to the table of contents for this anthology:

DeMarco, M. & Matthews, A. (2000)	Volume 9 Number 2	pages 48–79
Wallace, A. (1998)	Volume 7 Number 1	pages 58–89
Seidman, A. (2001)	Volume 10 Number 3	pages 76–83
Baek, S. (2011)	Volume 20 Number 3	pages 62–85
Graycar, M. & Tomlinson, R. (2010)	Volume 19 Number 3	pages 78–95

Book and cover design by Via Media Publishing Company
Edited by Michael A. DeMarco, M.A.

Cover illustration
Illustration courtesy of Bosco Seung-Chul Baek
www.chenbing.org

ISBN: 978-1-893765-12-2

www.viamediapublishing.com

contents

iv **Preface**
by Michael DeMarco, M.A.

vi **Author Bio Notes**

CHAPTERS

1 The Nurturing Ways of Chen Taiji:
An Interview with Yang Yang
by Michael A. DeMarco, M.A. & A. Edwin Matthews

32 Internal Training: The Foundation for Chen Taiji's
Fighting Skills and Health Promotion
by Adam Wallace

62 An Introduction to Seizing Techniques in Chen Style Taijiquan
by Yaron Seidman, L.Ac.

69 Dantian Rotation in Chen Taiji: Internal Energy
Techniques and Their Relationship with the Body's Meridians
by Bosco Seung-Chul Baek, B.S.

90 Tensegrity: Development of Dynamic Balance
and Internal Power in Taijiquan
by Michael Rosario Graycar and Rachel Tomlinson, M.Ed.

105 **Index**

preface

When we think of martial arts in "old China," we get visions of violent convulsions of dynastic change, devastating rebellions, civil wars, and banditry. Throughout the centuries there was a need for masters who possessed highly effective martial skills for positions in the military, protection services, and law enforcement. Out of this historical reality emerged a national treasure we call taijiquan.

Chen-style taijiquan formulated during the days of military strategist Qi Jiguang (1528–1587), and its founder is considered to be militia battalion commander Chen Wangting (1600–1680). The art evolved. Its mystique remains fundamentally a true fighting art, including bare-handed forms and applications, plus an arsenal of weapons that includes the spear, straight sword, broadsword, and halberd. Then there are the associated training methods used to master this complete system, such as qigong, push-hands, and standing post. All of these practices are infused with knowledge associated with the physical and mental aspects of the human condition.

Chen style encompasses a complete martial system. It has a deserved reputation for its combative efficiency, but also as a health-nurturing modality. The vastness of the Chen-style curriculum is way beyond the scope of most people to fully learn, so practitioners focus on what they can handle. Usually a solo routine is sufficient. Since all taiji styles stem from the original Chen family system, the Chens certainly share in the credit for taiji's popularity in general, especially as an exercise purely for health benefits.

Regardless of taiji style—be it Chen, Yang, Wu, Sun, Hao, or other—any serious taiji practitioner or scholar should have some understanding of the Chen family roots to get a vision of the whole tree. This two-volume anthology brings much of the rich heritage conveniently together for your reading. In this second volume, there is a special emphasis on nurturing the internal aspects for health as well as for combative skills. You will find clear explanations outlining each step in the learning process toward mastering Chen-style taiji. Chapters included here clarify what proper training entails and why much time and effort (gongfu) are necessary to gain results.

In addition to the detailed history and penetrating philosophy you'll find here, perhaps of greater importance are the clear explanations outlining each step in the learning process toward mastering Chen-style taiji. Only a very high-level teacher can understand what methods of instruction work best. Students don't know; that's why they should follow a teacher's instructions as closely as possible. Chapters included here clarify what proper training entails and why much time and effort (*gongfu*) are necessary to gain results. As echoed among practitioners in taiji's birthplace: "If you drink water from Chen Village, your feet know how to kick." This two-volume edition brings you to the village for traditional instruction.

                                        Michael A. DeMarco
                                        Santa Fe, NM
                                        August 2015

author bio notes

Bosco Seung-Chul Baek, B.S., has studied qigong and yoga, becoming a certified yoga instructor in 1999. He began studying Chen taijiquan with Chen Bing in 2002 and became a formal disciple in 2005. Mr. Baek attended Loyola University Chicago, where he received a B.S. degree in biology in 2009. He owns the Chen Bing Taiji Academy in Los Angeles.

Michael DeMarco, M.A., founder of the *Journal of Asian Martial Arts*, received his degree from Seton Hall University's Department of Asian Studies. In 1964 he began his martial arts study in Indonesian kuntao-silat; since 1973 he has focused on taijiquan. Mr. DeMarco studied under Yang Qingyu (d. 2002) in Taiwan, in the Yang-style lineage of Xiong Yonghe (1886–1981). He also studied Chen style in Taiwan under Tu Zongren and Du Yuze (1886–1990), in the lineage of Chen Yanxi. www.wingedliontaichi.com

A. Edwin Matthews started martial arts training in 1960 with judo and jujutsu. Since 1976 he has been studying taiji under William C. C. Chen (Yang style), Dr. Ping-siang Tao (Yang style and Liuhebafa), Peter Ralston (Cheng Hsin), and Dr. Yang Yang (Chen style). He earned a diploma of graduation from W. C. C. Chen. Ed has been certified in Dr. Yang Yang's Evidence-Based Qigong and Taiji programs.

Michael Rosario-Graycar has been studying martial arts on and off for over twenty-five years. In 1996 Michael started studying Chen-style taijiquan in Philadelphia, Pennsylvania, under Ren Guangyi, senior disciple of Chen Xiaowang. While continuing to train regularly with Master Ren, Michael also trains privately with Chen Xiaowang, Chen Xiaoxing, and Chen Bing. Michael currently owns and operates the Phoenix Martial Arts Center in Greater Philadelphia.

Yaron Seidman, L.Ac., graduated in 1993 from Guangxi College of Traditional Chinese Medicine in Nanning, China, and Auckland Acupuncture Colleges in New Zealand. He received national certification by the National Certification Committee for Acupuncture and Oriental Medicine. Mr. Seidman has a background in various internal martial arts and has focused on Chen-style taijiquan since 1999. He is a disciple of Chen Zhonghua and a private student of Feng Zhiqiang. Mr. Seidman teaches Chen taiji in New York City.

Rachel Tomlinson, M.Ed., has trained in Chen-style taijiquan for over ten years with Ren Guangyi, and has regularly attended workshops with Chen Xiaowang, Chen Xiaoxing, and Chen Bing, among others. Rachel serves as an assistant instructor at the Phoenix Martial Arts Center in Philadelphia. She received a M.Ed. in counseling psychology from Temple University in 2005. Currently, she works as the director of accreditation management for the Fox School of Business, Temple University.

Adam Wallace is vice chairman of the International Chen Style Taijiquan Association, Inc. He has studied Chinese cultural arts for many years. He is an authorized instructor of both Chen-style taijiquan, under Master Ren Guangyi, and Dayan (Wild Goose) qigong, under Master Michael Tse. Mr. Wallace teaches in New York City and Connecticut.

The Nurturing Ways of Chen Taiji: An Interview with Yang Yang

by Michael A. DeMarco, M.A., and A. Edwin Matthews

Photography courtesy of David Riecks.

Introduction

Taiji forms and styles are not all alike. There are different teaching and training methods involved. Plus, the overall reasons for practice may represent a wide-range of particular goals. It seems that a style's uniqueness is greatly influenced from the leading instructor of that particular system. If we look at Chen-style taiji, we find an array of sub-styles that reflect the flavor of individuals who have developed their own particular branch from the lineage. One of the more notable branches come from Grandmaster Feng Zhiqiang, born in 1926, who teaches in Beijing. We were fortunate to conduct an interview with one of Feng's direct disciples, Mr. Yang Yang, who provided an in-depth perspective on this particular system of Chen taiji.

The following interview was derived from two meetings with Yang Yang which followed workshops he conducted in Erie, Pennsylvania. These were held at Ed Matthew's studio called Body Awareness on October 12–15, 1998, and October 12–15, 1999. Yang told of how he became involved with Chen taiji at an early age and eventually became a formal disciple of Feng Zhiqiang. Feng has developed a clear, comprehensive way of teaching his system. Since Yang arrived in the United States to complete a doctoral program at the University of Illinois-Urbana, he continues to teach Feng's system to students here. The system is a balanced blend of the standard Chen taiji routines, locking techniques (*qinna*), silk-reeling (*chansijing*), push-hands (*tuishou*), and energy work (*qigong*).

Following the interview section is a technical section which illustrates some of silk-reeling exercises and locking techniques. It is hoped that readers will closely compare the movements shown in both these sections to find how particular segments can be found in both the silk-reeling and locking techniques. According to Feng and Yang, these same movements can also be found in the Chen-style routines, push-hands, and qigong since all work together for health as well as self-defense.

INTERVIEW

Yang Yang's Start In Taiji

■ **Where did you live in China and how did you learn about Chen taiji?**
I am from the city of Jiaozuo. It is about twenty five miles from the Chen Village, and so Chen style is popular there. Likewise, because the Shaolin Temple is just south of the Yellow River, Shaolin boxing is also very popular in my city. In the local parks you can see people play different martial arts. The interesting thing is that we can also see different versions of the Chen style. There are specific areas in the park where people practice their particular version and push-hands. It's a small city where people are very friendly. It's a good environment to start taiji study.

■ **What in particular attracted you to study Chen taiji?**
When I was very young, I had a health problem and got sick almost every week. I couldn't walk. I wanted to run and my face would get pale. The doctor said, "Don't do any physical education class. It will kill you." I was born in 1961. That was a difficult time in China. There were a high percentage of kids who were born at that time with health problems. We were not allowed to do any physical activity like basketball or soccer. Then a relative from Xi'an said, "You're lucky you stay so close to Chen Village. Why don't you try Chen taiji?" So, when I was twelve years old, I went to meet two teachers at our main city park. Later, they introduced me to a third teacher Zhang Xitang. They are all friends. So we just learned from each other.

■ **Who are these teachers and how did you meet?**
First I went to Master Wu Xiubao, who was a high-ranking official in our city. My mother was his secretary. When my mom took me to him, I had to wear very clean clothes and be on my best behavior. Then he looked at me and asked, "Ok, what's the reason why you want to study taiji?" My mom spoke, "You know he has a heart defect, but we don't have the money to do the surgery. This may help, so I rather you could teach him." He said, "I'm busy, but I will let my student teach him first." So actually I started with Master Yuan Shiming. Now Master Yuan Shiming is quite old. I think he is in his 80's.

- **Plus, all these teachers are good friends?**

Yes, it's amazing, the city, the people—the human environment is so good. There's no hatred, there's no complications, because there's no money involved. Just pure people that love the art. Usually students stay with one primary teacher, but sometimes the teacher will tell you to go to a particular teacher to learn something he excels in, such as push-hands or qinna. They will tell you, "Ok, go learn from this teacher" and introduce you to that person.

Photography courtesy of Larry Justinas.

- **Of these three teachers, which one was most influential for you?**

The most influential was the first one: Master Yuan Shiming. He was the one I studied with most of the time. He was very kind, very generous, and kept no secrets. Whatever he knows, he teaches you.

- **At the time of your introduction, did you have a concept of what taiji was?**

No, I just practiced. Every morning at 5:00 a.m. my dad got the stick "Get up, get out of bed, go to the park and play taiji." He said, "otherwise you're going to die. We don't have the money to send you to Shanghai to do the surgery. The only thing you can do is practice taiji." You have to go to the park at least thirty minutes before the teacher. You cannot be later than the teacher. That's rude. I would usually go one hour before. You make sure you do the homework before the teacher comes. Otherwise you would be embarrassed if you feel you cannot do what he assigned you.

- **After studying with him, did you have a pretty good overview of the Chen style?**

I studied with him seven years, but I cannot say I had a very good view of Chen taiji yet. I only got some basic idea of what to work on: the first and second routines, and some push-hands. The first couple of years we worked on the first routine before starting the second.

■ **Do most instructors teach the first routine to focus on relaxation?**

Relaxing is one aspect and obviously a starting point for beginners. Other fundamental exercises, such as wuji practice, are just as important to teach relaxation. All of the Chen style principles can be learned from practicing the first routine. If you do the first routine well, you can also do the second routine (*paochui*) and weapons forms well. If you have not learned the first routine well, your second routine and weapon forms will be just as lacking.

■ **Who did you practice push-hands with?**

I practiced with my taiji classmates. Sometimes with my teacher or his friends, who were teaching in the same big park. Sometimes we play push-hands with other teachers' students, too.

Photography courtesy of David Riecks.

■ **Did you practice push-hands through the whole period?**

After I finished the first routine. The reason teachers want you to wait a little bit is because they know that before we start learning taiji we already have accumulated stiffness in our whole body. Why learn to relax? We want to go back to our original condition in terms of relaxation. For example, a one-year-old or six-month-old baby is difficult to hold. Why? Because he or she is very relaxed. There is no stiffness there. As we grow older, we get more and more tense, mentally and physically. So we want to go to another extreme. But if you start push-hands at the very beginning it may make it worse. So this is why teachers say you should work on the form first.

■ **Are you usually left to practice by yourself?**

Most students go to the park every day to practice with a teacher. They just find a place near the teacher and practice by themselves. The teacher practices too. If students have a question, he would talk with them, show them a new movement, or make corrections.

- **If you couldn't do a particular movement correctly, what would the teacher do?**

It really depends on the teacher. In most cases, if the teacher is not happy, you would feel it. The only thing to do is go back and practice. It's not that you come to the park and that's the only time you practice. Practice in the morning, evening, during the day—you've got to do it. If you feel your are learning and improving through practice, then you go to the park regularly, otherwise you don't go back. That's what happens in a very traditional setting. There is not too much encouragement. Teachers just let you practice, practice, practice. Maybe sometimes they are happy inside, but they won't show it. They think that if they say too many good words you'll get a big head. They may say little so you will work harder.

- **Did you have any testing, or was it just day-by-day practice?**

There is no testing. Teachers just look at you and that's the test. They see you, they touch you, especially when you start doing push-hands. They touch you and they know. You cannot cheat them. That's probably what we can call testing—and it is all the time.

- **Do students practice for the first year or so mainly to learn all the basics regarding body movement and how the taiji movements should feel?**

Yes. First you've got to learn how your own body works. Then the teacher will tell you where you've got tension, where your alignment is incorrect, how to adjust your feet, and how to coordinate your body. You try to make the form correct based on his standards.

- **After studying with these teachers for seven years, you felt you didn't have a clear overview of Chen taiji yet. Did you finally feel more comfortable after meeting other teachers and seeing more practitioners?**

I would say there was a breakthrough after my teacher introduced me to Master Chen Zhaokui in 1980. That was a big turning point because Chen Zhaokui showed the applications, push-hands skill, and internal energy at a level of mastery I had never seen before.

- **You then traveled to study more?**

I went to study engineering at a college in Shanghai. Because my dad is a musician, he believes if one wants to learn how to play music well it is always good to visit the best teachers. However, even though someone is a well-known or famous teacher that does not necessarily mean that he really understands the art. You should be able to recognize that. The more you visit, the more you can compare and learn. So he always encourages me to visit teachers. So I applied that idea to my taiji practice. Plus, I'm lucky I had good teachers to encourage and help me. They helped me a lot. For example, my first three teachers are all friends of Chen Zhaokui. They learned from him so I also got the opportunity to learn from him. I did this whenever I went back to my hometown on my summer vacation from Shanghai.

- **Did Chen Zhaokui study with Chen Fake in Beijing?**

Yes, Chen Zhaokui is Chen Fake's son. He lived in Beijing for most of his life. Later, he spent a lot of time traveling and teaching taiji in other cities. So people from Chen Village invited him back to teach. And the younger generation from Chen Village studied from him. Unfortunately, he died when he was pretty young. I think the reason he passed away had a lot to do with the political stress.

- **Your next teacher was Feng Zhiqiang? How did you meet him?**

In 1982, I attended a national taiji conference in Shanghai called "Famous Taiji Masters' Gathering," or something like that. I met Master Feng there. What happened was that one of my hometown teachers, Zhang Xitang, also went to Shanghai to see the gathering. He was a good friend of Chen Xiaowang and asked him to try to introduce us to Master Feng. We just wanted to see him. So one day during the seminar, Chen Xiaowang called to say, "I talked to uncle (he called Master Feng "uncle," because Feng is one generation older), and he would like to meet you guys."

- **You must have enjoyed this special gathering and seen many taiji styles?**

I loved it very much. That was the first and last biggest master's gathering in China to this day. That was the first time in my life to see so many top masters from the taiji community. Most of the best teachers of all taiji styles attended. It was hosted by Gu Liuxin because he held a good government position and had the power to arrange the gathering. People respected him because he was a scholar and was good in martial arts. For Chen style, they had Master Feng, Hong Junsheng—another one of Chen Fake's recognized students—Gu Liuxin, and Chen Xiaowang. For the Yang style, they had Fu Zhongwen and Yang Zhengduo. For Wu style, they had Ma Yueliang and his wife, Madam Wu, plus Wang Peisheng. For Sun style, they had Madam Su Jianyun.

There were some others as well. With such masters giving presentations and demonstrations, this event offered people a very rare opportunity to see the different styles. I am not aware of any similar meeting taking place before or since then. Perhaps in the future there will be another.

■ **You left Shanghai to go to school in Beijing. How did you make time to study with Master Feng?**

During the last year of engineering school, in 1983, I was thinking about quitting college and just devoting my life to taiji training with Master Feng. I talked to him about it and he said, "No, finish your degree. Just finish your work, and I'll try to get you a job here in Beijing." Getting a job is the easy part. In China, the problem is to change *hukou*, the local registration that everybody must have. Because my first job was in Shanghai, my huko was in Shanghai. There was almost no way for me to transfer my hukou from Shanghai to Beijing. That was a big problem. Master Feng did help me and I tried very hard, but it didn't work out. The only way was to go to school, so I went to law school in Beijing. I skipped a lot of classes and instead went to the park to practice. But I did do well and passed the national bar examination in 1988.

■ **In which park does master Feng teach?**

It's called the Temple of Heaven. That park is very unique because of the numerous evergreen trees—most of the Chinese martial artists believe you can get lots of energy from evergreen trees. So we usually do qigong there.

■ **You practiced there early in the morning?**

Yes, early in the morning. I would usually get there about 6:00, sometimes 5:30. You just have to arrive there before the teacher does.

■ **It is interesting to hear you would go to class an hour to forty-five minutes before the teacher arrived.**

Even now in China for many social activities and even work, some people may be late. But as part of taiji training, it's a moral obligation to be on time. Especially in traditional training, you may find a knowledgeable teacher, but they don't have to tell you anything. They may want to see if you are always on time and make it regularly to class. They want to know if you are really serious before accepting you as a student or not. What they teach is very valuable. You've got to treasure it.

■ **If someone wants to study with a particular teacher, how would a teacher establish the relationship?**

Before you begin studies they may investigate you to see if you are a nice person, work hard, and whether you respect old people. The respect of old people is a primary criterion on their list. They say if you don't treat your parents well, you are not a person they want to be affiliated with. Teachers say, "If you do not treat your parents well, how can I teach you? How are you going to treat me?" It's very simple logic. So they may investigate that, and investigate how you treat your friends. They may teach you some basic exercises and movements and, in the meantime, they test you.

TEACHING THEORIES

■ **You studied at first for health. Why not Yang style?**

There's no doubt Yang style is more popular than Chen style—than any style. But people can start with any style. Whether you have access to a teacher may determine the style you can study. If you can get access to all the different styles, then it's easier to choose which version you like. With Chen style, you can start with any physical condition, background or age. I've been working with people who started in their 70's and they are doing very well. Some people have misunderstandings about Chen style.

■ **Some say Chen style is for fighting and Yang style is for health and the elderly.**

Yes, I really want to talk about this. I'm not being critical of other styles, because any style may be good if taught by experts in that style. The key issue is whether you get the real stuff from your style or not. If I practice Chen style but I couldn't get the real stuff I'd say, "Chen style is not good" that's not fair, right? My point is that health and self-defense or fighting are actually one issue. Usually people separate the two— "I practice for health," or "I practice for fighting." I don't think that's the method for understanding taiji better. Such a division won't lead to a complete understanding of taiji practice. If you are not healthy, you can't fight well either.

Taiji is such a rich practice with so many benefits. Beginners cannot comprehend the wealth it contains. All aspects of the training system are related. You cannot say "I want this but not that." If you study only one part, then your returns will be considerably less than if you understand and practice the complete art. Why limit yourself from the beginning?

■ **So the primary thing is to work on being healthy?**

If you keep yourself healthy, then you can fight and you can defend yourself. That's really about internal energy. That's taiji practice. Working on your internal energy and getting stronger is good both for your health and for your self-defense. You can use it for both.

■ **When you started teaching here, did you find that students wanted to progress faster, learn more and more movements, without giving the basics enough attention?**

Like taiji, Chinese martial arts, Beijing opera, music, you may have to follow their rules. You have to start from the very beginning, otherwise nobody would teach you. You have to follow their rules from the very beginning. That's good for you, because if you don't have the foundation you cannot go to a higher level. Yes, most of the students want to learn more and more forms, so they feel they are making progress. As teachers, we should point out to the students the importance of the quality of the form and the basics, which include qigong and theory.

Photography courtesy of Larry Justinas.

■ **Can teaching be adjusted to the individual so they can progress according to their own abilities?**

Yes, in fact it should be that way in all aspects of training. We talk about the individual, their personal background, and physical and mental condition. In taiji, we talk about yin/yang: there should be some variations as we follow the principles. Going back to one of your other questions about the different versions of Chen style... People have different understandings of the art.

The art is so rich; maybe you look at it from one angle and I look at it from another. As a result, we have a different understanding. It is more important to incorporate the principles. For example, it doesn't matter whether one practices taiji with a big frame or small one. The version may be different, but the principles should be the same.

There's an old saying in China, "First you copy, then you want to try to change." At first it's not easy to see how to do it—you make a copy. Like in the feeling of push-hands, even when you talk about hard/soft, you really have to touch the teacher; you really have to feel it. So this is one of the subtle parts of taiji training. You cannot get this even on videotape. I really have to touch to know what the teacher means. And even if you touch, you still have to think very hard.

■ **Because you can still misunderstand the touch?**
Yes. Theory, form practice, and applications must be combined. We can get the feel of a movement or a technique, practicing it over and over so we can learn something and understand it better. Then we can talk about it. It is important to copy the movements. Even subconsciously, I can always learn from my teacher. Then we talk about including applications.

■ **Applications? Does this include all the variations?**
I think it's not good for beginning students to have too many choices. They should make a choice, and then consistently do the same thing so there's no confusion. Later on, students start to see the other possibilities. "How about moving this way? If I'm going backwards, I could use my elbow instead of my fist?" But if you just start with one application, it is easier to build from there.

■ **How are the concepts of hardness and softness in Chen style explained?**
There's one old saying from the classics: "Accumulation of softness will lead to hardness." We do need both, soft and hard, but we cannot start with hard. We need to accumulate softness and then transfer the softness to hardness.

■ **What is softness? Do you need to put your hands on an experienced teacher to know?**
To make it simple, softness is being relaxed. And here I want to make it very clear the differences between softness and collapse. The two are completely different. A lot of people make the mistake of collapsing when they try to be soft. You have to feel it. You cannot learn it from a book, you cannot learn it from a video tape, or CD. Yes, you have to feel it. Personal touch and feel.

■ **What does it mean to be double-weighted?**
There are two ways we can understand this. One is purely physical weight distribution. So if we use this standard, it would be fifty percent on each leg, right? As long as we have a 50/50 percentage, we're double-weighted. But there's another way to understand this—it is whenever you lock yourself. If you can't move easily, you are double-weighted. Even if you have 60/40 percent distribution, you can still be double-weighted. As long as you cannot shift your energy from one point to another point, you have double-weightedness. That's my understanding.

■ **What do you mean exactly by "locking yourself"?**

Locking your energy flow within the whole body. If you feel it is difficult to move lightly and quickly, you are "locked." Even if my physical weight distribution is 50/50, but I can move my energy quickly with agility, I am not locked. Alternatively, if my weight is distributed 80/20 but I cannot move my energy from one point to another, I am locked.

■ **Some people have not completed copying a system from a competent teachers. Then they start to invent new movements or systems.**

I think this is why there are different styles such as Yang, Wu, and Sun. Of course, the safest way is to study a recognized style that has stood the test of time and/or was created by a recognized master in his initial art. Creative students have obtained the basics by copying; then they combine with their own personal experience from other martial arts. They create different styles. But they have to study very hard for a long time. They have the ability and the knowledge. In America, most people don't have the patience to finish the first stage, so they probably won't be able to develop a new system.

Photography courtesy of Larry Justinas.

■ **When compared with China, many teachers in the United States have a limited background in Asian martial arts. How can we progress?**

One of the advantages here in the U.S. is that there is more exposure to high quality Asian martial arts, especially now that people can come here from China. They also bring the culture and understanding with them. The good thing is that communication in America is very open. America is a rich country and people have the technology and means to learn. More and more, the top teachers of different styles are traveling to America to teach or give seminars. Communication and sharing of ideas is occurring at a much greater level than ever before. Most people work and have a family and don't have a lot of time to practice. The key is to make the practice as efficient as possible.

I want to be realistic. In China, in the old days, there was a saying that "you must be rich to study martial arts." The meaning was that most people didn't have the means to travel to see a teacher or spend time practicing. You don't have to be rich, but it is no easy task to reach a high level of gongfu, and it does require sacrifice. It depends upon how hard you try, how serious your practice is, how well you can truly understand and apply the principles in your daily practice. For any student, whether in Asia or America, there is also fate.

As long as we keep trying, we'll get the chance to meet some people who can really teach something worthwhile. For example, take my case. In 1980, Chen Zhaokui came to my hometown to teach. I was very lucky because my teacher knew him and introduced me. Unfortunately, I only had a short time with him before he passed away. I also had a chance to take private classes with Chen Xiaowang. He had to come to my city to take the train to Beijing. When he stopped here, he visited his "taiji uncle," Chen Zhaokui. Chen Zhaokui said, "This is my top student Chen Xiaowang," as he introduced me. Not long after that, Chen Zhaokui passed away.

In 1981 or 1982 at the National Taiji Gathering, Chen Xiaowang introduced me to Master Feng. In my hometown area, people talked about studying with Master Feng and Chen Zhaokui because they were the top 18th generation Chen-style representatives. My dream was just to meet them. I didn't think I could learn from them. It was just fate. When masters like Feng meet a new student, they check the student's personality as the training progresses—if they are respectful, whether they improve, whether they train hard—these kinds of things. Then they will decide whether they will take him or her as a formal student.

Shanghai is a good place for martial arts study. When I was in college there, I often went to visit Gu Liuxin. Master Gu was the president of the Shanghai Martial Arts Association. He was a very knowledgeable scholar, very kind and open. He would always say, "Master Feng's push-hands is the best." It's not easy to become his student because he is also very tough.

■ **In the United States, many think they can become "masters" in two or three years. Do you think this is possible?**

The "quick-learn masters" may be very smart, but nobody can be smarter than the accumulation of four or five hundred years of experience. You may be smarter than two generation's accumulation. Your technical experience may accumulate greatly in one generation and you may feel you have exceeded the skills of the old masters. But this is impossible because the members of the "family" lineage have devoted all their energy and lives to this art. I made similar mistakes too. In 1981, 1982, and 1983, I entered the Shanghai College martial art tournaments and took first place each year. However, after I met Master Feng I realized that actually I knew nothing.

■ **One student was practicing a movement and I asked her what she was doing.**

She said "pushing," but her body was moving backwards as her hand moved forewards. I stood in front of her and asked her to push me, and of course it didn't work.

As a practitioner, I should know what my focus is and what I'm doing. You gave a perfect example of a very common misunderstanding of technique. Simple physics must be understood. For example, in movement my body may have twenty pounds and my arms have five. If they move together in the same direction, I can get twenty five pounds applied to the subject. If they are moving in opposite directions, I may get negative fifteen pounds. If my body moves backward, I may end up with only five pounds of pressure moving to the front. But if my body also moves in that direction, I end up with twenty five pounds. It's pretty simple physics. What happens to some people is maybe the teacher passes on misinformation or maybe the student's understanding is wrong.

■ **If someone has studied one martial art and watches another style, they think, "I know that technique." But perhaps they really do not.**

The technique should be essentially the same among different styles of taiji. Just make sure you really understand the style you are practicing. If possible, try the same technique from other styles. It will enhance your understanding. The technique is not fixed. Most people think, "I've learned one technique; it will keep me safe." One very good thing to find out about the whole training system is that it is limitless. For example, with qinna you can really make one technique after another. From one qinna, comes a counter qinna, then another qinna. If you become static, it does not work. Likewise with silk-reeling exercises and the Chen routines. So the silk-reeling, the routines, the qinna, the counter qinna, and qigong—all work together all the time.

■ **Some people who are very busy with family or their work have only limited time to practice. Are there basic things that you never want to skip? Is there a priority?**

I would say, don't skip qigong. If you are busy, still do the qigong. If there is more time, then practice the routines and silk-reeling.

■ **Silk-reeling after the routines?**

The silk-reeling and the routines are almost the same rank. After that, you learn push-hands. Push-hands is not only an exercise for you to consume energy. It can also be used to generate energy. That's a very important point. As long as we can make our practice more energy-oriented, no matter what we practice, we'll be okay. So why mention push-hands? Because lots of people think push-hands is just pure energy consumption. That's wrong. With push-hands, you should train in a gentle nurturing way. You can train to generate energy instead of purely wasting or consuming your energy.

■ **What type of qigong practices would you recommend? Standing pole?**

Yes, standing pole is one static part of qigong practice. There is also the dynamic, or moving part. Start with the standing, and then later you can do some moving qigong exercises.

Photography courtesy of David Riecks.

■ **Is any particular type of qigong good for beginners? Are all the same?**
There are many styles of qigong. Like any other profession, you've got good and bad instructors, especially in qigong. People want quick results. Based on that demand, some people create strange exercises that are bogus. It has happened in China and I expect it's going to happen in the United States, or already has happened here. So I want to take this opportunity to say to the readers in your journal: be careful and make sure you're practicing correct qigong. Because this is something unlike the taiji routines. Practicing the routines incorrectly may hurt you, but not too bad. But, if you practice qigong the wrong way, you may cause great damage.

■ **How many different types of exercise are there in qigong?**
We do stationary qigong, including standing, sitting, and even lying down. Our routines, silk-reeling and push-hands practice are dynamic qigong. As long as we can use it to generate more energy, it is qigong.

With push-hands there are a variety of exercises. You have two-person exercises with stationary feet, using a single-arm or a double-arm engagement. You have two-person exercises with moving steps.

■ **In qigong and silk-reeling practice, what should we visualize? Should we look for a certain feeling or sensation? Or, should we simply practice and wait to see what happens?**

Many different experiences comes from qigong practice. It can be the feeling of becoming extremely small or huge. It can be very hot. It can make one side cold, or one side hot. It can cause trembling in the dantian. You may see some other person appearing huge. You may feel that your whole body becomes very light or you become very happy. I would say, don't pursue this kind of thing or try to get this kind of experience. If you don't have this kind of feeling, it doesn't mean you are doing it wrong. You are okay. But if you pursue that kind of experience, you may have problems.

In my case, I had the feeling that my whole body was sinking into the ground. But my other taiji brothers and sisters had other experiences. There are a couple of criteria you can utilize: keep it simple and be natural. You can try the different versions of qigong, but don't fool yourself. Don't believe people who say they can send you energy, or you don't have to practice. You've got to do the work yourself to be your own healer. You are your own healer. We've got to do the work. Practice, but first try to make sure the things you get are correct. Improve with practice, and then keep working.

■ **How does it benefit our taiji by having our inner energy flowing?**

In general, when we watch someone perform taiji, we usually ask if the taiji is "empty" or not. Is there energy there or is it just pure mechanical movement? An experienced teacher can check a student's energy flow in different ways, such as through push-hands, or just looking at the form. After you start practicing an internal art, it becomes very easy for you to see what energy is in the form.

■ **Just like in calligraphy and other arts?**

Yes. It has content, feeling, and meaning. When you express yourself, you can really express it through the energy. I told my father, who is a musician: "Dad, people ask me, 'When you play taiji, why is it different every time?' And I tell them because it feels different." And I say, "That's from my music training." The art is yin/yang. Some part is high, some is low—one dynamic exchange between yin and yang. That's art. So I would say, in order to understand taiji, if we have time, study other arts. And that will come back to help us understand taiji better. All arts are closely related.

■ **Most think that qi will make them powerful. What is the role qi development has in improving one's taiji practice?**

According to Chinese medical theory, everybody has qi. It is one of our training goals to make our qi strong and balanced. It should come very naturally. A lot of people ask to see it. I really cannot let you see it, but when we try push-hands you can feel what that means. Here's another issue: Some people say that "The only people to fully develop their internal qi are special people, like monks on a misty mountain who train for fifty years." I would say no. Everybody can cultivate their qi. If you get the right form and practice the correct way with dedication, you can improve your qi. You can do it for your health, push-hands, and self-defense.

■ **If somebody is very good in qigong, but never practiced push-hands, they probably would not do well in push-hands. They have to be healthy and also know the whole-body movement?**

Good qigong, form, and silk-reeling will help you to know yourself better. Push-hands practice helps you to understand both yourself and your partner. You need both. It's a choice. You've got to do the routines, do the silk-reeling, and you've got to apply your qi in these practices. That's true.

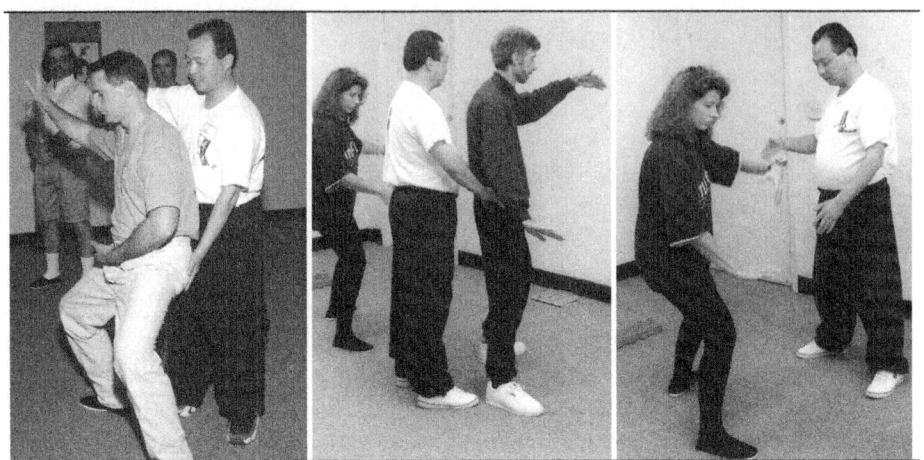

Photography courtesy of Larry Justinas.

■ **Is qigong study one way to learn how the body works? And also how the qi circulates, opening meridians so that the qi flows naturally?**

Yes, qigong can also help us understand how our body works. The qi will flow naturally through the meridians by itself. The best way always is to be natural, letting it go by itself. Qigong generates more internal energy, making your qi stronger, and improves qi circulation in your taiji practice.

■ **A beginner usually starts with qigong or the first routine?**

That depends on the teacher. Some like to start with qigong and others start with form. We must pay attention to cultural differences too, because generally people have an idea that taiji is a morning exercise for the elderly. They already have an image of taiji in their mind. So when I came to the United States and started teaching, I would ask, "So you guys think that is what taiji looks like? Let's try this."

After they got involved, they really enjoyed it. Then I'd say, "Here is the whole training system. Do you want to learn the real stuff?" After they practice qigong, they can easily tell the difference between only doing form and doing both (qigong and form). Then they can tell the difference between qigong and taiji and are happy to practice both. Recently, with the help of the media, people are getting a better understanding of taiji and qigong.

■ **How do you compare your teaching methods with Master Feng's?**

There are different levels of taiji training in terms of weight shifting, coordination, footwork, silk-reeling, etc. It is difficult for beginning students to study, practice, and get the benefit if they start with the refined level. So, I first present the essential form and silk-reeling. Gradually, based upon the student's progress, I will introduce the more subtle, refined movements and silk-reeling. I refer to these levels as "essential" and "refined" forms. This method has been working very well. Every time I meet with Master Feng, I realize I still have so much more to learn. His system is so very rich. That's the biggest difference between us. There's also a small difference. I live in America, so I probably know American culture a little bit better than my teacher. So in terms of how to present things, I needed to change the teaching method a little bit.

■ **What makes up the whole system as Feng teaches it?**

Master Feng's system is truly unique. It includes the Chen-style first and second routines, and many single form repetition practices. For example, he teaches static qigong (standing and sitting qigong), dynamic qigong exercises called Hunyuan Gong, silk-reeling exercises, push-hands drills, and sparring gong. There are about ten basic gong routines. I should say the thing his system focuses on most is being very natural. Second, it's scientific. What I mean by scientific is that the system always emphasizes nurturing. The whole process of practicing is to nurture yourself. That's his very unique process. That is what makes his taiji so powerful. His techniques are unique.

In order to nurture, you have to train in many aspects, like qigong and diet. Another important point is to pay attention to your emotional stability through spiritual training. Maybe you practice the first routine as training. So why practice qigong, and why have a moral standard for disciples? This is not only for moral reasons, but also for the art. Can you imagine a fighter, if he loses his temper all the time? If he always wants to hurt other people or doesn't have a peaceful mind? There's an old saying in China: "Ten thousand things come from quietness." Peacefulness comes from peace. By being quiet, we can accomplish ten thousand things in our life. We believe health and even fighting skills are highly related to one's moral, emotional and spiritual being. These are applied to taiji study. It's not pure technique or practice. Because Master Feng talks about spiritual nurturing, physical nurturing, and diet nurturing, I feel that his system is very unique.

■ **He is very different from the other teachers you have trained with?**

Yes. You asked why I chose him as my teacher. Number one is fate. Also the criteria I used to choose a teacher is by what he really knows. How I check this is by looking at his disciples to see if they're good. And I look at his practice to see if it's good or not. Another criterion is to see if he is willing to share his knowledge with me. Of course, you yourself should be good and pass his test. But, assuming you pass his test, will he share his art with you or not? Because no matter how good the teacher is, if he doesn't want to share his knowledge with me, there is no reason to call myself his student. So, I think Master Feng is a very good person, plus he's knowledgeable, and he's willing to share with his students. So I chose him.

■ **That is a valuable part of his system. How does Master Feng work with students' characters? Is it all indirect?**

He himself sets a good example for the student. He treats his teachers, taiji brothers, and even his neighbors very well. I was staying at his home when I traveled to Beijing, so I saw these relationships. Second, sometimes he would tell you some stories to teach you. I would say nobody is problem free. I have personal problems, sometimes very serious problems. I talk with him. He sometimes talked about applying taiji principles to our work, politics, and even personal crises. He is really a *shifu*—a teacher-father. He teaches you lots of moral values, instead of only, "here's the first routine, second routine, go ahead, do it," and then you graduate. Like the last time I went to Beijing, the first thing I must do is go see the teacher. It's what a son would do. For two years when I worked in Shanghai at the college, I traveled in the summer and winter to Beijing to train with him. The travel expenses took all of my money, so he let me stay with him at his house. You have the feeling that if you don't practice hard, you feel guilty—you have that kind of feeling.

YANG'S TEACHING METHOD

■ **What is your reason for teaching Chen style and what keeps you going?**

I feel a responsibility, an obligation to share my experience with the people here, and maybe sometime back in my country. I started taiji practice because of poor health and it made me physically and spiritually strong. How these physical and spiritual aspects work together and how can we get more people to get the benefits—these are the big reasons I switched my academic major to the field of kinesiology.

A lot of people have skills that are much higher than mine. But not too many people felt as strongly as I did about taiji after it cured my health problems. So I would like to share this. This is why I attempted to study kinesiology even though I didn't have any preparatory background. It is very hard for me to study this, but I think I can go forward. There's more research to be done in Chinese medicine. I need to study more of that, too. I need to study more physiology, biology, and anatomy to see whether we can really understand this art better.

■ **Your own personal research?**

Yes. I am very fortunate to conduct research under the guidance of my advisor Dr. Karl Rosengren, Dr. Eddie McCauley, and Dr. Rick Washburn leading professors in motor learning, exercise psychology, and exercise physiology. We are all excited about our preliminary research results and plans for future studies.

The other thing is the learning process. Everything moves together; it's one big thing. We can get many benefits from taiji training for the beginner, intermediate, and advanced practitioners. The more I study taiji, the deeper it seems. This includes how we apply taiji in our daily lives to handle our problems, such as financial, political, or whatever. It's very rich. More and more people also want to get the spiritual benefit from it.

The first World Congress on Fighting Sports & Martial Arts was held from March 31 thru April 2, 2000 in Amiens, France. This photograph was taken during a reception held on April 1st at the mayor's office. Left to right: Dr. Willy Pieter, Michael DeMarco, Dr. Karl Rosengren (Yang's academic advisor), Yang Yang, and John Heijmans.

■ **What information and skills would you like a student to take home from your seminars?**

First, to understand that each part of the practice—the routines, qinna, qigong, push-hands, and silk-reeling—are integral aspects of the whole system and are closely related to each other. These different parts are not isolated. Second, to focus on learning the twelve essential taiji principles as taught by Master Feng. The third thing is that I hope, by giving examples, that people can learn to apply the taiji principles to their daily life. This is the real benefit people sometimes don't recognize. Daily practice is important to gain benefits. For example, applying the principles can alleviate knee and shoulder problems which are pretty common now. People can look at the Chen-style routines, applications, and silk-reeling exercises to understand any martial art style better. And also how we transfer our form and push-hands exercises to qigong exercises.

■ **Between an intermediate and an advanced student, is there a difference in emphasis, refinement, or in technique?**

Taiji is such a rich art, it is almost impossible for beginners to fully comprehend the potential benefits. Differences in level are relative—how can you draw the line between "intermediate" and "advanced"? There is a famous Chinese saying: *shan wai you shan, tian wai you tian*, which means after this mountain there is another mountain bigger and higher, after this world there is another, bigger world. So, how can you say what is "advanced"?

This said, I can answer your question in a general way. I would consider my "intermediate" students to be those who know the basic form and have begun practicing the refined movements, silk-reeling, and push-hands and also have reached a certain level in qigong. I can check their gong by touching them in push-hands and by looking to see the energy in their forms. I have been teaching in the U.S. for six years now. I would say that, in this time, I do not consider any of my students to have reached an "advanced" level. Beginners practice the first routine in a slower manner and higher postures than advanced students. Over time, when appropriate, they may increase speed and move into lower postures. At the beginning stage, it is important not to try to make the postures too low.

The beginner just builds the basic structure. On the side, we practice the silk-reeling and even simple push-hand drills. Then, we proceed to bring these together. For example, through silk-reeling we obtain more meaning in the form. We use silk-reeling to generate more energy to supplement qigong practice, which also refines our form. Refining one aspect helps refine the others.

■ **Do you find push-hands practice is the best way of learning sensitivity?**

It's part of the training. We cannot say it is the best way, because the whole curriculum, the whole training, includes the routines, silk-reeling, qigong, and push-hands. All of these should work together.

■ **Some say that all you need to practice is the routine. If you are ever attacked, you will automatically be able to defend yourself.**

There is a reason why all of the different elements are included in the training system. The training curriculum was developed for some reason. Why do people practice the routines, qigong, qinna, and push-hands? There must be some reason. I would suggest that people will make better progress if they practice the complete system. It's better for us to try and see what happens. Some people practice twenty or thirty years and, when you touch them, they don't have the skills they should have. There must be some reason.

If you try just one year, or even six months—try the push-hands, silk-reeling, and qigong exercises—see what happens. See whether that can make some difference for your progress.

■ **Do you feel it is important to learn the applications of each movement while you're learning the routines, or learn them later?**

Learn the applications along with the movements. Actually, most of the movements have more than one application. But we should know the basic energy. For example, when we talk about the preparatory form, you have the *peng, lu, ji,* and *an* energies. Everything there is very clear. If you don't know the basic energies you can make some progress, but not as efficient as it's supposed to be. So understanding the basic energies is a requisite for understanding the we should know the basic applications for of each movement.

■ **So if you teach the first routine, do you teach one application for each movement?**

Not for every movement, just for most of them. Basically, you should tell people what basic energy is there in terms of *peng, lu, ji,* and *an*. Because when we do push-hands, that's basically the application of *peng, lu, ji, an, cai, lie, zhou, kao*—especially during stationary push-hands. These are the main forces, therefore we need to train these forces. So when we do the routine, I think we should understand the *peng, lu, ji,* and *an* basic energies so it can make more sense for the practice. Like with the *an* energy, if you try it whenever you practice qinna, or push-hands, or whatever, you can apply it.

■ **Are there variations in the routines?**

Variations come for different reasons. Big variations arise because of differences in understanding the theory of the principles, and on personal training and experience. There may be some good or bad variations. It's difficult for people to judge which one is good or bad. My suggestion is to visit different teachers, then compare and see whether the thing you get is correct or should improve, because there's no way you can judge by yourself. If you cannot see the difference, how can you compare? So I would say, read books, go to different seminars. That doesn't mean you do not respect your teacher, now. You really love the art; that means you love your teacher more.

■ **You have a variety of martial artists attending your workshops, but each seems to find something to help their own practice.**

Whatever you're practicing, see through the workshop whether you can get something maybe you missed, maybe your teacher missed, from the Chen system. Like the silk-reeling. Any style has "white crane spreads wings." If you add silk-reeling, see the energy there? Even that much makes a big difference. You don't have to change your style. You can get some things from the workshop. That's what I think—especially the silk-reeling. Lots of people have knee problems. The problem happens because people have too low of a posture too early in their practice, or they hold an incorrect posture which may hurt their knees. Also, their alignment may not be correct. People twist a lot. The foot and the knee should be consistent with your body's direction. These two things help a lot of people in my workshops. I'm very happy with that. Some people just do the form the wrong way. They come from different styles, not only Chen style. We do need to move the knee, but the range of motion should be reasonable. That's one big thing I like about Master Feng system: nurture!

PEOPLE

Chen Xiaowang	陳小旺
Chen Zhaokui	陳照奎
Chen Zhaopei	陳照丕
Feng Zhiqiang	馮志強
Gu Liuxin	顧留馨
Hong Junsheng	洪均生
Wu Xiubao	吳秀寶
Yang Yang	楊楊
Yuan Shiming	原士明
Zhang Xitang	張喜堂

CITY

Jiaozuo	焦作

TECHNICAL SECTION

SILK-REELING

The 1a–e series shows a single-hand exercise where the right wrist turns in a counter-clockwise direction. This can be reversed in a clockwise direction with either hand.

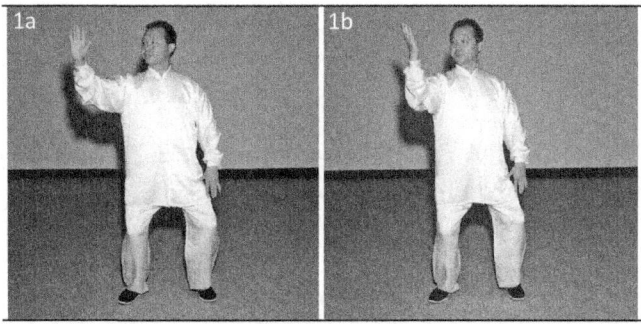

The 2a–c and 3a–c series are double-hand exercises with the wrists moving outward (2) and inward (3).

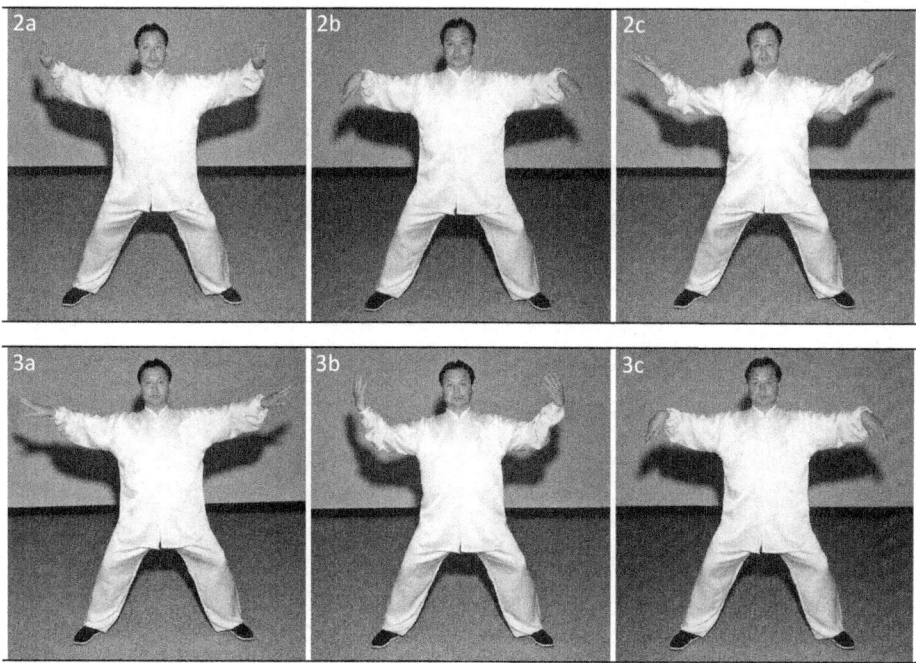

The 4a–f series involves moving the right arm in a circle while shifting the weight. From 4f. drop the right arm and shift into the 4a posture and repeat. Practice with the left side also.

SILK-REELING

The 5a–f series is similar to the preceeding 4a–f series, except the rotation is done with the elbow circling.

SILK-REELING

The 6a–f series commences with both hands held in fists to the sides. They then cross in front of the navel and begin to circle upwards. You can see a rising of the waist as the legs slightly straighten. The arms continue to circle outward to the sides. The body sinks downward in unison with the arms' downward movement to their original position.

QINNA

In the following examples, two defensive locking techniques are shown. Yang's right wrist is grabbed from the same side in the 1a–d series. He moves his left hand over the top of the grabbing hand to hold it in place. As this is secured, he rotates his right hand over the opponent's to bring pressure on his wrist. The opponent sinks in an attempt to relieve some of the pressure. If Yang continue to apply pressure in a downward motion, the opponent would go to the floor in submission.

The 2a–d series is similar to the 1a–d series except the grab is done from the opposite side with the opponent reaching with his right hand for Yang's right wrist. Again, Yang secures the grabbing hand with his own left hand. This time, he circles his right hand clockwise around the opponent's wrist having the same result.

COUNTER-QINNA

Counter-qinna offers a way to respond to a locking technique with another locking technique. In the 1a–d series. Yang grabs his opponent's right wrist. The opponent moves into the wrist lock technique shown previously in the 2a–d series. With his left hand, Yang secures his opponent's hands while relieving the pressure on his own wrist by circling his right elbow upwards then onto his opponent's arms. As Yang sinks downward, his opponent is locked and placed off-balance. This makes it easy for Yang to shift into a shoulder-push.

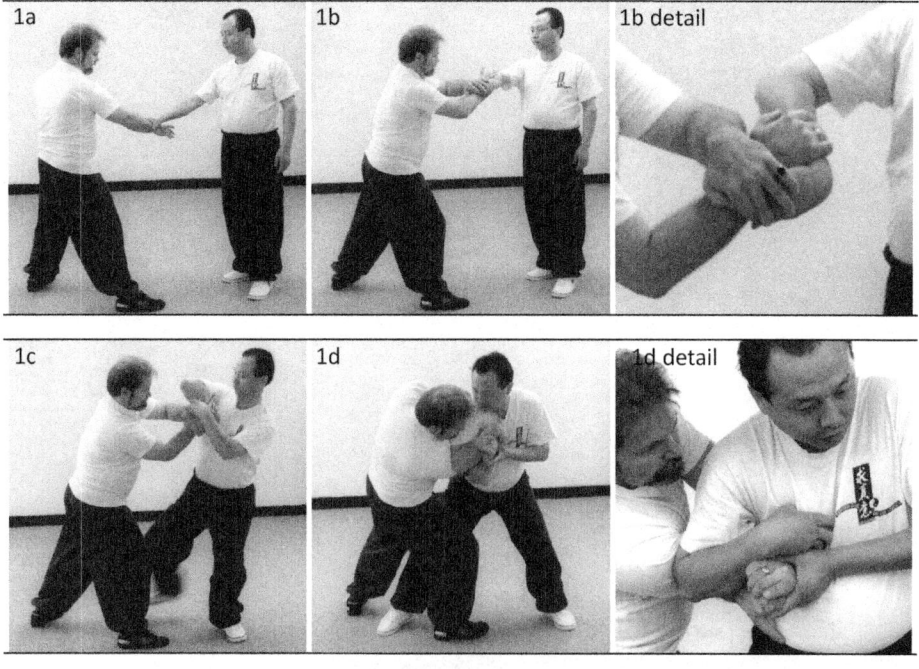

Photography courtesy of Larry Justinas.

Yang demonstrates three ways to counter a lock when pressure is applied to the wrist as the elbow is held (2A–B–C). According to what he senses, he first moves to render the lock ineffective and then throws the opponent either forward (A), past his right side (B), or downward (C).

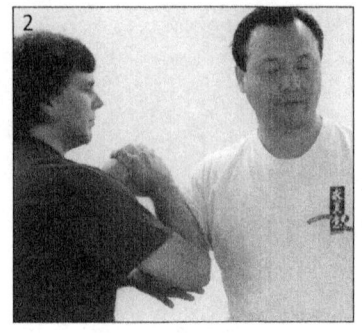

COUNTER-QINNA

Yang shows a simple counter to an upper-arm hold (3a–c). He turns his own arms outward which causes the opponent to loose the security of his grip. At the same time. Yang shifts forward to push his opponent off-balance.

In series 4a–h, a grab is countered with a counter-qinna as shown previously in the 1a–e counter-qinna sequence. Yang follows the counter-qinna with another counter by sinking and moving into a forward push.

COUNTER-QINNA

Yang shows a defense against an upper arm grab or push in the 5a–d sequence. Rather than placing strength against strength. Yang counters by pushing his opponent's arms slightly outward to break the foundational source of his opponent's push. He then steps in to push the unbalanced opponent backwards.

In the following sequences. Yang manipulates a one-hand push against his chest (6a–c) and against his stomach area (7a–c). Both are countered in a similar fashion by securing the opponent's elbow to secure the arm. This allows Yang to lock the opponent's forearm which applies pressure against his opponent's wrist. As the opponent withers in pain, it is easy for Yang to step forward to throw the opponent.

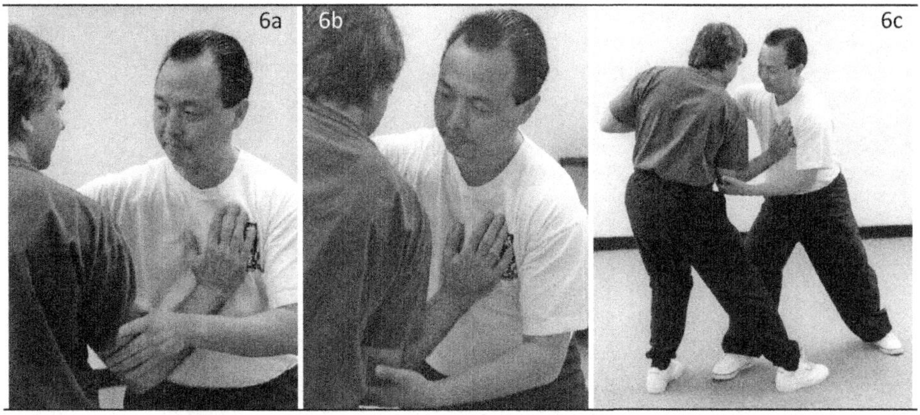

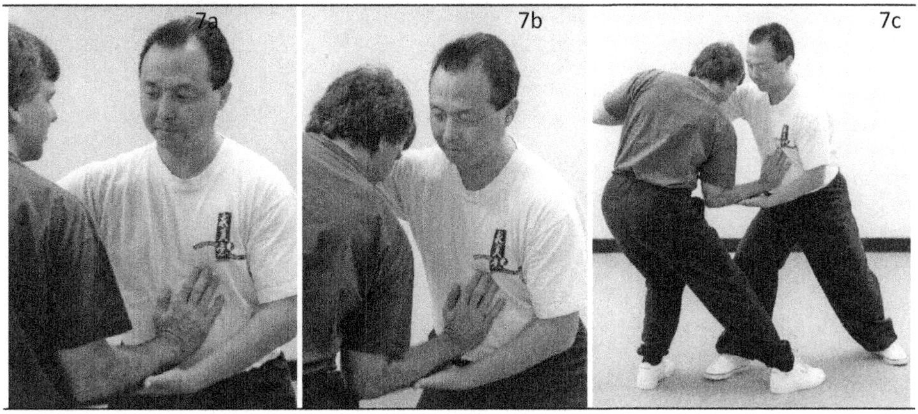

Concluding Remarks
The technical section provided on the previous pages is an attempt to illustrate how silk-reeling and qinna practices are interrelated. The circular silk-reeling movements can be found in locking techniques and counters, as well as in the Chen-style's solo routines and energy work (*qigong*).

Internal Training: The Foundation for Chen Taiji's Fighting Skills & Health Promotion

by Adam Wallace

Reversal of a qinna technique by Ren Guangyi.
All photographs courtesy of Adam Wallace.

Today in the Western hemisphere taijiquan (also abbreviated as taiji) for combat is really something of a contradiction in terms. It has become a "moving meditation" or a martial arts dance at best. The fact that taiji boasts a comprehensive fighting system for self-defense and full-contact offense when there are so few practitioners of the art aware of this fact is a great anomaly. The explanation for this discrepancy, and how it has come to be, can be found within taijiquan's evolution.

Taijiquan's Origins and History

In the 1930's an eminent martial arts master and historian named Tang Hao (1897–1959) concluded after thorough research that taijiquan had originated in Chenjiagou (Chen Village), Wen County, Henan Province, over three hundred years ago. Its founder, Chen Wangting (c. 1600–1680), was a knight and scholar and a ninth generation ancestor of the Chen family. He was chief of the civil troops around 1640 at the end of the Ming dynasty (1368–1644). According to the genealogy of the Chen families, he was renowned as a "born warrior, as can be proven by the sword he used in combat," and a "master of martial arts having defeated over one thousand bandits in Shandong province." In 1644, after the Qing dynasty came to rule China, Chen Wangting returned to his village where, in addition to working in the fields and teaching disciples and children to become worthy members of society, he began creating his new "Grand Ultimate Fist." He invented this system as a means of training warriors in a healthy, wellrounded manner from his life-time of researching, developing and experiencing martial arts.

Painting of Chen Wangting,
probable creator of taijiquan.
Chen Xiaowang in sword posture
Golden Roosters Stands Alone.

The original Chen taiji was created as an eclectic martial art embodying the most empirically tested techniques from General Qi Jiguang's *The Canons of Boxing*, an effective and powerful repertoire which covered sixteen different martial art schools. Qi Jiguang (1528–1587) lived some fifty years prior to the advent of taiji. From *The Canons of Boxing*, Chen Wangting created five sets of taiji shadowboxing, one set of Longboxing (108 forms) and one set of Paochui combat boxing. These incorporated skills from Shaolin Fist, the Red Fist in particular, Shaolin Staff, and "Buddha's Warrior Eighteen Grasping Techniques" in addition to other boxing and staff techniques. He added to this foundation special techniques from other famous masters of the time, such as Li Bantien's legwork, "Eagle Claw" Wang's grasping, "Thousand Falls" Zhang's take-downs, and Zhang Baijing's striking. These individuals, all masters of their respective arts, were equally as celebrated as General Qi Jiguang.

Historically, Chen family boxers were essentially bodyguards required to protect valuables and transport them across neighboring provinces, especially Shandong province, which had endured a long history of turmoil. The Chens relied on their martial skills, specializing in the sword and spear, not only for their survival but also for their livelihood. Their skill was a closely guarded secret, and for five generations it had remained intact within the family and village.

Chen Changxing (1771–1853), the fourteenth generation patriarch, was the first to teach it to an outsider, Yang Luchan (1799–1872), who came to Chenjiagou for the sole purpose of learning taiji. Yang had previously only studied external gongfu but his tenacity impressed Chen Changxing. He was taught under the condition that he would vow never to teach the art to the public or use its name. After a time he traveled to Beijing, where he become known as "Yang the Invincible," and true to his oath, formulated his own shadow boxing. His Yang-style taiji was based on Chen's *laojia yilu* (old frame first routine). He omitted the stamping, explosiveness, low postures, and changes in tempo characteristic of Chen taiji, as well as the more difficult motions, in order to make it easier to learn and perform, and to suit it more for keeping-fit purposes. This style soon became popular and was embraced by the masses.

After several revisions to the original Yang forms, Yang Chengfu (1883–1936), Yang Luchan's third grandson, adapted and created the large frame of Yang family shadowboxing. This is the most popular form in China and the world today, with its slow tempo and extended, graceful and circular movements.

Ren Guangyi and Chen Xiaowang
perform Lazily Tying Clothes (*lanzhayi*)
from Chen's old frame routine.

Wu Jianquan (1870–1942), having learned small frame Yang taiji from his father (who studied under Yang Luchan), taught this style, which became known as Wu Style. The frame is very compact, performed with uniform slowness, and contains none of the leaps and jumps that exist in the Chen school. It is the second most popular style, next to the Yang style. Another Wu school evolved around 1850, unrelated to the first mentioned Wu clan, with their own brand of taiji, which derived from Chen-style laojia (Yang Luchan's version and the Chen's new frame from Chen Qingping [1795–1868]). Its emphasis was on body structure and inner power. This was adopted by Sun Lutang (1861–1932), already an expert in *xingyi* (form-mind) boxing and *baguazhang* (eight trigram palm), who combined the best of these three styles and formed Sun-style taiji. These five styles comprise the largest and most noted styles of taiji in the world today. Directly or indirectly, Chen's new frame, Yang, Wu, Wu, and Sun all have their origins in Chen's laojia yilu.

Due to the simultaneous advancement of firearms, the function of martial arts on the battlefield gradually became obsolete. Yao Hanchen, a scholar and a student of Yang Luchan, questioned the role of taiji and proposed that it was to "enhance longevity and extend radiant good health into old age." This view brought the transformation of fighting art into health exercise.

In China, "shadow boxing" is a valuable health exercise and has had remarkable success as a curative for neurasthenia, neuralgia, high blood pressure, heart disease, tuberculosis, arthritis, and diabetes, among other conditions, due to its deep regulated natural breathing, relaxed frame of mind, and smooth circular movements (*chansijing* or silk-reeling energy) which contribute to dredging the acupuncture channels and collaterals (*jingluo* and *jingmai*), as well as to improving the functions of the skeleton, muscles, and lymphatic and digestive systems. Taiji, in having diluted the martial aspects, has lost its original essence over the generations. Chen taiji, however, has seen the least amount of change as a martial art, yet through standing pole training (*zhanzhuang*) and silk-reeling exercises (*chansigong*), detailed in this article, it offers one of the most comprehensive systems of qigong, or internal training for health, available.

Until very recently, Chen taiji was perhaps the least known of the major styles, largely because it remained within Chenjiagou. Ironically, when Chen Fake (1887–1957) was invited to Beijing in 1928 (after Yang Luchan had introduced his Yang taiji to the public) and performed Chen taiji, it was scarcely recognized as taiji, with its intense focus, release of power, stamping, etc., as the public was already familiar with the slow and gentle form suited for the elderly practitioners of the art.

Now that it is being more widely spread around the world by masters directly from Chen village, interest in taijiquan's roots is booming. While the majority of the other styles have almost completely lost their combat capability, Chen taiji has always remained a martial art. But it should be duly noted that even within Chen taiji there are relatively few teachers who have a high enough level of proficiency in the combat arts to teach them.

One such teacher exists in the United States. His name is Ren Guangyi (b. 1965), and he studied directly under Chen Xiaowang (b. 1946, the nineteenth generation standard-bearer for Chen family taiji) full-time for ten years, to become Chen's top disciple. Chen Xiaowang now has thousands of students all over the world and travels ten months of the year giving seminars, but there were only four main disciples studying together in the beginning. When Chen Xiaowang left China and emigrated to Sydney, Australia, Ren headed West and brought the genuine high-level skills of Chen taiji with him to America.

The rooting power of Chen Xiaowang as he withstands the push of seven men.

Chen Xiaowang and his signature.

Evolution Within the Style

Chen Changxing, the fourteenth generation master, created the two barehanded sets, *yilu* (first routine) and *erlu* (second routine). Yilu is a fusion of the first three routines created by Chen Wangting. Yilu provides the foundation and prepares the student for push-hands (*tuishou*), joint-locking (*qinna*) techniques and some light wrestling.

Yilu is considered eighty percent internal and twenty percent external, with its use of "issuing power or explosive energy" (*fajing*), which is to say that the form is intrinsically more soft than hard. Erlu is a synthesis of the earlier Longboxing and Cannon Fist routines and prepares the student for free-fighting. This form is eighty percent external with its emphasis on increased fajing, speed, footwork, leaping, dodging, elbow and shoulder strikes, footsweeps or leg-takedowns, and sudden changes of direction. The first form is to build up the practitioner's vital energy (*qi*) and concentrates on developing stability, with focus on silk-reeling energy (*chansijing*) and the eight skills or energies (*bafa*):

1) *peng*: "inflate/ward-off," used to intercept and control an opponent's advance;
2) *lu*: "rollback/pull downwards," to deflect and control an advancing opponent;
3) *ji*: "press/follow," dropping and rotating in contact with the opponent;
4) *an*: "push," pressing one's weight into the opponent;
5) *cai*: "pluck," or grasping and twisting an opponent's joints and extremities with maximum force;
6) *lie*: "split," creating a torque of two opposing forces within the opponent's body, such as stepping in and throwing from behind, or trapping the opponent's body between the practitioner's leg and a pivoting arm or shoulder;
7) *zhou*: "elbow strike"; and
8) *kao*: lean, or striking with the shoulder, knee, or hip.

Pinyin	Wade-Giles	Chinese
an	an	按
cai	ts'ai	採
ji	chi	擠
kao	k'ao	靠
lie	lieh	挒
lu	lü	履
peng	p'eng	掤
zhou	chou	肘

In tuishou and combat, these energies are frequently used in combination.

The second routine is for total combat and vast amounts of energy are expended performing it. Traditionally it was believed that one's training was not complete unless one studied both bare-handed forms, as the emphasis in each is quite different.

The legendary seventeenth generation master Chen Fake (grandson of Chen Changxing and grandfather to Chen Xiaowang) created *xinjia*, or new frame, which is widely practiced in China and the West today. This too comprises an yilu and erlu, and laojia was used as its blueprint. Xinjia was created to enhance the family's fighting skills. Chen Fake added more detail, making both of the forms longer, and designed his new frame to be more compact, and to contain more complex chansijing, more fajing (with more places from which it can be issued) and more qinna techniques, rendering it more useful in practical application and combat situations.

In addition, there are other subtle differences between the two renditions. For example, the stepping in laojia tends to be more forward on a straight line while in xinjia the stepping is more at oblique angles. Xinjia has become the more prevalent of the two and is certainly the preferred form in competition in mainland China, due to its more flowery, expressive style, and dynamic nature. Laojia and xinjia are the same style and share the same root, with the same principles, but the latter is more difficult to learn and perform, and so the former is generally taught first.

A common mistake with many practitioners of the new frame is that they have a tendency to exaggerate the spiraling movements, which results in the appearance of excessively large, flaccid circles and loops, causing the individual parts of the body to become separated from the waist. Those practicing taiji in this manner fail to grasp the principles of chansijing, which are far more subtle, and more internal than external.

The most recent addition to Chen family taiji is Chen Xiaowang's simplified thirty-eight-movement solo form, a combination of laojia and xinjia which contains many of the fundamental movements, but less of the more difficult ones and less repetition of movements. It takes a shorter time to learn and perform (between four and five minutes) than laojia (approximately ten minutes) and xinjia (approximately fifteen minutes). The thirty-eight movement form has become very popular throughout China and is hailed as something of a triumph by taiji beginners.

Ren Guangyi in Buddha's Attendant-Warrior
Pounds the Mortar (left) and Single Whip.
His name brushed by Chen Xiaowang.

The Main Sources of Chen Taijiquan

Taiji was intended to be more than just a fighting art. Chen Wangting combined the external martial techniques with the ancient methods of *daoyin* (guiding qi down to the *dantian* or lower abdomen) and *tuna* (deep breathing exercises from the dantian). Both of these health preserving skills, which date back to fourth century B.C.E., later combined and evolved to become what is today's qigong.

Chen Wangting developed his martial art with careful attention to the jingluo–jingmai channels through which qi flows. The purpose of this is really twofold. On the one hand, knowledge of jingluo–jingmai theory enables the practitioner to effortlessly attack the qi of the opponent's internal organs. On the other hand, the spiraling, twining, and arcing movements (characteristic of Chen-style taiji) which originate from the *dantian* (or lower abdomen) are primarily for opening these channels and encouraging the natural flow of qi, to cultivate the health of the practitioner. If the dantian is strong and open, the individual will be healthy and possess vitality.

It is because taiji is trained with the knowledge of the workings of the inner body and combined with breathing that it is often referred to as an "internal" martial art. The taiji boxer's consciousness, movements, and breathing are all interrelated. Many people do not really understand the concept of "internal" so it is generally assumed that because taiji is an internal art it must be soft. This is a mistake. By definition, "taiji" must embody both soft and hard. This is why Chen taiji has an external set—erlu, better known as Paochui or Cannon Fist. When one has witnessed this form performed correctly there can be no doubt as to whether or not taijiquan is wholly "internal."

In addition to the eclectic fighting techniques, deep breathing, and jingluo–jingmai theory, Chen Wangting also incorporated the ancient Daoist yin-yang concept, the universal principle of complimentary opposites, which forms the foundation of Chinese culture and philosophy. Within the scope of taijiquan, yin and yang refer and relate to: opening and closing, firm and yielding, hard and soft, expanding and contracting, fast and slow, ascending and descending, solid and empty, etc.

Regarding the legs, yin and yang are most important. The weight must be clearly distinguished to avoid double-weighting. This is not the same as balancing the weight or having the weight equally distributed throughout the limbs (as in zhanzhuang or the Preparing Form in any of the routines). "Double-weighting" means that one's body is in a position that is not readily mobile because the weight is not properly placed. To develop a strong root, one leg must be full and support the body while the other leg is empty and can move in any direction. When stepping one must move like a cat; the weight should not be transferred until it is safe to do so. If one needs to retreat, one should be able to withdraw the leading leg without any disturbance to the balance or any shift in position or height to counterbalance the movement. According to Ren Guangyi, many taiji practitioners do not transfer their weight properly, therefore limiting their self-defense skills.

Yin and yang also applies to the upper and lower body. If the legs are firm, strong, and solid, then the upper body must be correspondingly relaxed, loose, and empty. This softness is needed for developing sensitivity which is necessary for the fostering of "listening or awareness energy" (*ting jing*) needed to sense the opponent's intentions. The slightest movement by the opponent after contact has been made with the arms should be read by the taiji practitioner, as his body is like a scale. With the legs providing the base, the upper body is light, with a feeling that the head is suspended from above. Light and heavy or rising and falling should be measured to the slightest degree. When the practitioner's silk-reeling energy is good, he will react with just the right amount of energy, which means that he will not break his own energy and lose balance. Too little in counter-attack will be rendered ineffective and too much may cause the practitioner to lose his root by overextending. The right amount requires great subtlety. If the opponent does not move, then one should remain still. One should feel the opponent as he shifts his position, no matter how slightly, and uproot him while his weight is in transition, i.e. yin and yang are unclear. Through the practice of chansigong, one's energy becomes more refined and one's sensitivity increases. Eventually, one's reaction to the opponent when he advances or retreats will never be premature or too late, and one's neutralization skills will be honed to perfection.

Understanding yin and yang in defense is paramount. If the opponent resists a qinna technique (a major feature of Chen taiji) for example, it is no use to resist his will and struggle for domination. Instead, adhere to him where contact has been made and when he moves follow and borrow his energy to collect and strike. If he is yang, then become yin and change direction or revolve. If the opponent pushes, one needs to pull, and vice versa. If he attacks with the left fist, all the qi is concentrated in the left arm, so it becomes yang, or strong. This means that his right shoulder, arm, and fist will be yin (weak or empty), so that is where one's attack should be directed. Knowledge, understanding, and application of these principles leads to the ability to spontaneously implement the famous taiji principle "four ounces deflects a thousand pounds" and to taijiquan mastery. Ren Guangyi explains: "It is like trying to move a bull. Push it. It will not move. But tie a rope through its nose and pull, then it will come quite peaceably. It is a matter of reading energy, which comes through repeated practice of the forms and push-hands." Form and push-hands practice are dependent on the basic training exercises called standing pole and silk-reeling, both explained in detail below.

The Poem of Chen Wangting

It is ironic that today taiji is generally thought of only as a "gentle martial art." The earliest recorded taiji poem is Chen Wangting's "Song of the Canon of Boxing." Within the verse he outlines many techniques and fighting tactics. It may astonish many people that he writes, "Two round kicks smash the face, then with left and right side kicks" and "Covering the face to attack the body is known to everyone, but striking the heart and elbowing the ribs are uncommon." This type of aggression may seem barbaric to those who practice taiji solely for relaxation and health or to those who appreciate only the aesthetics of the art, as a form of self-expression or an expression of Chinese culture. However, one's thoughts must always return to the simple fact that it was created as a martial art. It is undeniably a healthy exercise but it was not created solely for this purpose. Those who are interested in taiji for health only may eventually receive greater health benefits through the practice of qigong, which is purely for health and longevity and has been in existence several millennia before taiji.

Left: Split (*lie*), creating a torque of two opposing forces within the opponent's body. the photograph shows Master Ren, after stepping in behind his opponent, throws him from behind. Right: Ren's left hand locks the opponent's wrist while his right arm coils under the opponent's elbow, which then acts like a fulcrum.

Chen Wangting advocated using every part of the body in attack, or whichever part was in contact with the opponent's body at any given time. In his poem, he refers to "attacking (feinting) to the left and striking the right," and the element of psychological surprise, such as feigning retreat only to suddenly change direction and stop the enemy in his tracks (breaking the enemy's rhythm). This is in addition to techniques such as "chopping, punching, pushing and pressing, dropping, blocking, grasping, hooking, opening, closing, dodging, rolling, tying, sweeping," etc.

There are five groups of sparring techniques within Chen-style taiji:

1) *leg techniques*, which include kicking, hooking, linking, sweeping, and stamping;
2) *striking*, namely with the hand, elbow, and shoulder;
3) *fajing*, which includes *cunjing* or 'inch energy,' short-range power;
4) *joint-locking*, often used in combinations with the other techniques; and
5) *wrestling*.

So, while taiji develops sensitivity and is generally thought of in connection with yielding and redirecting, it can also be extremely aggressive, a characteristic not typically associated with this martial art.

Most of the experienced and seasoned (non-Asian) taiji practitioners in America today are the "old-guard" who grew out of the 1960's and early 1970's "peace movement" (when taiji became popularized here). Many of them were fuelled by antiwar sentiment and/or under the influence of illegal substances. As a result, they did not possess the "warrior spirit" which belonged to their Chinese predecessors and is needed to fully develop the skills to become an indomitable fighter. Many also dislike Chen taiji for this reason and are not willing to readily accept that the art they practice descended from a pure fighting style. This attitude reflects that of a large number of practitioners and instructors today. This generation has further contributed greatly to the dilution of taiji, as a combative art.

Left: Pluck (*cai*); grabbing and twisting
the opponent's arm with force.
Right: Completion of the cai technique.

Basic Skill

Excellence in taiji comes only from daily repetitive internal training. To practice correctly and achieve the results of a firm unshakable root, heightened sensitivity, the ability to neutralize from any position, internal strength and explosive power, takes hours of hard practice every day for many years. The work involved does not merely refer to sweat but also to pain. It would be a delusion to think that a high level can be attained any other way.

Generally Western students of martial arts differ from those in China. The majority do not have the time, patience, or the inclination to put in the hours needed. Many are either too lazy or too content to spend even minimal time practicing, and often basic skill is omitted in favor of forms. As a result, few achieve levels of mastery. Hence the overall standard of Western practitioners is not as high as in China, and this only strengthens the case against taiji as a combat-oriented art today.

The following describes some of the basic training techniques for Chen-style taiji, namely the standing pole (zhanzhuang) and two methods of silk-reeling (chansigong). Standing pole is a very common form of static qigong, usually practiced as if holding a ball with the eyes closed. However, Chen-style standing pole can be practiced with the eyes closed or open. This exercise enables the practitioner to gather qi and strengthens the muscles and bones. The silk-reeling methods within the Chen repertoire, some practiced stationary and some moving, are too numerous to be listed here. The following are the first two basic stationary skills as taught by Chen Xiaowang. The first trains single-hand silk-reeling while the second trains double-hands. No matter what style of taiji one may practice, these exercises will only enhance one's level of skill.

Standing pole and silk-reeling are essential to taiji's practice for health, but also to its martial capability. Both are superb exercises for health in their own right, especially the standing pole, practiced by millions of Chinese, many of whom do not practice any martial art. In Chen taiji training, even though standing pole and silk-reeling constitute the basis of forms training, they are never to be disregarded, even later when the practitioner becomes advanced. The principles adhered to during standing relate directly to the form's practice, i.e., head kept upright, shoulders relaxed, chest concave, hips sunk, etc. and are retained throughout the routines. Standing pole and silk-reeling are integral to developing a stable root, powerful legs, and relaxed and sunken hips (needed for an open, low, and comfortable stance), as well as a relaxed and calm frame of mind.

Above: Chen Xiaowang demonstrating application of laoji yilu at a seminar in New York. Below, left: punching with fajing. Below, right: Single Whip posture.

Practice of all these above characteristics leads to the proper development of fajing. True fajing is not mere brute strength but internal power—a sudden, relaxed and fluid explosion of force. Many attempt to imitate it, either through making excessive noise exhaling while striking, or by simply vibrating the fist upon full extension of a weak punch. In these cases either too much external force is used, or there is no power at all. Those that rely solely on their might only become stiff. Fajing is only possible through the correct alignment of the body, proper relaxation in the posture, and the sudden transference of weight from one leg to the other.

Ren Guangyi practicing a
Chen-style sword routine.

Standing

Standing in the manner described below is really a dynamic tension exercise for the legs and is crucial for qi development. For health, the practitioner does not need to stand very low, but to develop taiji as a martial art one must sink lower. Leg power becomes fortified as the practitioner learns to sink and relax. Mastery of this exercise comes from learning to relax with a painful pressure placed on the legs. As the legs are solid (yang), the upper body must become empty and relaxed (yin) to achieve balance. In the beginning stages this is difficult to achieve, but the more time one spends actually 'standing' the easier it becomes to relax. The intense pressure comes from within and is, therefore, completely under the practitioner's control. It all depends on how low he is prepared to sink. When he feels too tired or has endured too much pain, he can simply raise his posture until such time when he is ready to sink again. To the casual observer this exercise may not look beneficial, but internally circulation is increased, hormones are stimulated, and he may well wonder why the practitioner who appears to be doing nothing in particular perspires so profusely, despite no shortage of breath. The object is to assume control of the internal pressure, strengthen the internal organs, calm the mind, and develop strength without physical effort by the musculature.

As the body sinks and the degree to which the knees bend increases, the tendency is for the knees to extend forward beyond the toes or for the upper body to lean forwards. This is common among practitioners, especially beginners, or those who have no teacher to correct them. This bad posture removes the burden from the thighs, where it should be, and places it squarely on the knees, which can result in damaged ligaments. To compensate for this, one must sit slightly backwards. (However, this does not mean to lean backwards.) The problem then becomes one of balance. It may seem awkward and uncomfortable in the beginning but eventually this becomes easier through correct practice. The key is to relax and open the hips.

In the beginning, the main difficulty with standing pole is disciplining oneself to sink more and increase the pain threshold, and to stand still for increasingly longer periods when the mind is used to activity and constant stimulation. The idea is eventually to relax completely and forget everything and enter a mild meditative state. Thus the qi will sink to the dantian and flow more strongly, passing through the entire body, causing the practitioner to feel calm, clear, and energetic. Once the body is still, the mind neutral and balanced, the spine relaxed, and the dantian's qi balanced and strong, the body internally becomes like a "taiji painting," according to Chen Xiaowang.

Wuji and Taiji

Standing pole is also known as wuji standing. The Chinese believe everything comes from *wuji* or "nothing" (an infinite void) and then becomes taiji or "something." When it does become something we have the One (taiji). The famous Chinese yin/yang symbol embodies this concept. Taiji is the circle, the One, the condition before yin and yang. It is a common Western misconception that taiji and yin/yang are one and the same. Taiji is moving, dynamic and chaotic. Only when taiji settles does it separate to become Two (yin and yang). Once One becomes Two, this gives birth to the Four Dimensions which divide to give the eight situations (*bagua*), which provide the sixty-four hexagrams (*pa*) as detailed in the *Yijing* (*Book of Change*), which holds the formula for divination. It is believed that everything in the universe is symbolically represented within this book, and can be divined by understanding the hexagrams. Taiji is the principle or concept on which the eight trigrams and the *Yijing* are based.

Taiji is the martial art based on this philosophy. Thus, following the Dao (nature), wuji should be practiced before taiji. In other words, stillness is developed before movement. We follow nature by practicing wuji first and then when the qi is strong from having been accumulated, we can begin to use it in preparation for silk-reeling and the taiji forms. Thus balance is maintained between yin (stillness) and yang (movement).

Chen taiji is physically very demanding and consumes vast amounts of energy because of its low postures and especially the use of fajing. This is even more apparent in erlu (second routine), also called the Cannon Fist. Erlu, which is geared more towards full combat boxing, is the antithesis of yilu (first routine) and is predominantly an internal form. Chen family taiji is the only style of taiji boxing which has a second empty-hand routine. This tremendous energy must first be cultivated and stored in order to be used, otherwise the practitioner would become exhausted. This is the purpose of standing pole and silk-reeling. In fact, many practitioners of erlu who have failed to follow the principal safety rules concerning internal development have injured themselves and suffered many unpleasant side-effects, such as nausea, fainting, retching, and, in worst cases, some have even coughed blood. Taiji without internal training would cease to be a health-giving martial art.

When one stands still long enough, focuses internally, and closes the door of the senses to all external stimulation, one will develop an increased awareness of the body, and eventually come to gain sensitivity to movement inside. Externally the body is static but internally the heart is beating and the qi is flowing. This is the condition known as "motion in stillness." During the practice of forms, externally there is activity, but internally one should be very calm relaxed and centered, and the mind should be still. This is the condition known as "stillness in motion."

Stillness in Motion and Sensitivity

Internal sensitivity is only possible through becoming yin: internally focused, mentally still, relaxed, calm, and receptive. If the posture is not correct, the flow of qi will be impeded and one will be unable to relax, which will inhibit not only the sensitivity of the individual to his own internal workings, but also to the energy of his opponent. In Chen Wangting's 'Song of the Canon of Boxing' is contained the line, "Nobody knows me, while I know everybody." This refers to the practitioner's sensitivity to an opponent's energy and intentions and the simultaneous ability to conceal his own intentions. The way to know the enemy is to know oneself first.

Chen Wangting also created the two-person training exercise known as push-hands, whereby practitioners' arms make contact and press mutually with the idea being to conceal one's own movements so that the opponent has no way of knowing whether one is opening or closing, to be wholly unpredictable, as through twisting and coiling together one uses sensitivity to read the opponent's movements and foretell his next move. This is a high level of martial art because one is not required to merely block incoming force with force but to follow the opponent's energy to defend oneself.

The fighting skills are raised to a higher level through silk-reeling where, according to the poem, "power comes from within" and "inner energy becomes outward power." In the early stages one should aim to stand for a minimum of ten minutes. The time spent on standing pole should be increased gradually. According to Ren Guangyi, serious taiji students should spend between thirty minutes and one hour. For the first six months of his preliminary training, all Ren did was this painful standing. His teacher has been known to 'stand' for two hours. The longer one can accomplish this task, the stronger one will be and the better one's taiji will become.

The principle of taiji is not to force anything, so a weak person should practice building up slowly. For many people who practice taiji solely for health purposes, ten minutes may be sufficient. But to develop taiji as a high-level martial art, standing must be done for long periods and this can be painful. As the object of push-hands and combat is conquering an opponent, it could be said that standing pole is for conquering oneself.

Silk-Reeling

Chansijing (silk-reeling) actually takes its name from the silk worm itself, as it manufactures silk in a coiling motion. The external movements of the taiji form resemble the work of the silkworm as it creates silk. The purpose of silk-reeling as health exercise is to strengthen the body and open the dantian through the turning of the waist and to smooth the *jingluo/jingmai*. In taiji all of the energy is generated from the dantian. Silk-reeling prepares the practitioner for forms practice and strengthens the body through its coiling motions.

Left: jingmai; right: jingluo.

The martial application of the silk-reeling exercises comes through teaching the student to move in circles until this becomes instinctual. The first half of the circle is used to neutralize or redirect an opponent's attacking force and the second half is for counter-attacking the opponent, using (borrowing) his own force against him. When the silk worm first ejects the silk from its body the single strand of silk is very fragile, but after it's wound around a branch numerous times it becomes extremely durable and resilient as it has been amply reinforced. This same principle is applied to the human body. For his efforts, the dedicated practitioner will achieve the physical quality most often associated with the great taiji masters, that of "steel wrapped in cotton."

The silk-reeling practice involves a flow of uninterrupted sets of movements. The purpose of this is to keep the qi flowing, to prevent it from becoming blocked. In martial usage, this capacity enables the practitioner to flow and regain his center when he is pushed. This is the neutralization capability of silk-reeling.

Most people become stiff when they are pushed and their qi becomes blocked, causing the body to lose its connection with its center and waist. If the incoming force is greater than their root, they will lose their balance because the ability to neutralize has been lost due to the dantian and back having become tight.

When the center of gravity or the center-line is struck or pushed, the individual tends to lose equilibrium. Repetitive practice of reeling silk prevents the qi from becoming blocked so the center can always be preserved. High-level skill involves the sensitivity to be able to change jing internally and reposition the body so that the center is never in this vulnerable position. The dantian is constantly shifting, or at very least, it is always in a stable position where it is able to change when the need arises.

On the health level, according to traditional Chinese medicine the body's healthy functioning depends on naturally free flowing qi. When the qi becomes blocked along a specific organ network the corresponding organ will be adversely affected, causing the whole body to become ill. The channels need to be dredged and kept open. Silk-reeling keeps the qi flowing and opens the channels. This is the exercise's primary goal.

The main principle when practicing silk-reeling exercises is to be natural and relaxed. Turn the waist and allow the hands to follow. It is a grave mistake to use force to push the qi along. This will only arrest the development of the looseness needed to reach a high level. All silk-reeling movements originate from the waist and involve the dantian and the *mingmen* acupoint (on the lower back directly opposite the dantian) and require the cooperation and coordination of the whole body. When the waist spirals, this creates spiraling movement through the shoulders, elbows, and wrists to the fingers. As the hips, knees, ankles, and feet are connected to their upper counterparts, silk-reeling movements pass down through these joints to the toes and return to the dantian.

There are millions of taiji practitioners throughout the world. Not all practice silk-reeling. Those that do not are only able to use up to fifty percent of their body's capacity to accomplish any individual movement or strike. This also means that when they need to use power or fajing they will only be able to use fifty percent or less of their power. Mastery of silk-reeling enables the practitioner to utilize his entire body into a concentrated, focused strike with an effortlessness that most practitioners of taiji can only dream of ever achieving.

The Requirements of Standing Pole

The head should feel as if suspended from above. One can imagine that there is a light object on top of the head and to prevent it from falling one must remain very still. The chin must be slightly tucked in so that the *baihui* point (crown of the head) is facing the sky and connects with the *huiyin* point (inside the legs, between the reproductive organs and anus). The hearing should remain concentrated behind so that the qi will sink to the dantian. In this situation the mind should be very clear. The chest should feel loose and relaxed, which will make the dantian feel full. If the abdominal muscles are tight and the dantian is tense it will close. This means that the qi cannot pass through the dantian. In this case it will become lodged in the chest and cause a feeling of tightness or oppression in the chest which, in turn, will increase the burden on the heart. This situation can be remedied by a simple readjustment of the posture.

The fundamental goal of standing pole is for the entire body to support the existence of the dantian and not the stomach muscles. When the arms are held at shoulder height *peng* energy is developed. This is an important quality, used for warding-off and for maintaining distance or space between oneself and an opponent. The effect of this should be like an inflated tire. *Peng qi* is best described as the power of resilience and flexibility. Of all the eight methods (*bafa*) associated with taiji, it is the most important essential energy. A taiji practitioner should always have peng energy. It is the energy of defensive attack, used to evade and adhere. This energy is used when moving, receiving, collecting, and striking. With peng qi, the body reacts like a spring which rebounds when pressed. If an opponent applies pressure and ones arm folds, peng qi has been lost, and so has ones best line of defense. Often during standing the arms begin to feel tired and ache. In this case, you can lower the arms to waist height but keep them extended (see photo 5 in the silk-reeling double-hands exercise #2 in the technical section) which develops the qi at the dantian, or just bring them closer to the body at shoulder height, making the circle smaller. When the shoulders and arms once again feel comfortable, return them to the original position.

In the beginning stages, it is common for the legs to shake and burn. In fact, there is a traditional saying in Chen village, "Whosoever drinks the water of Chen village, their legs will shake." As the legs become stronger, standing in this manner becomes more comfortable and one may even come to enjoy the sensations that accompany standing pole practice. When the strain on the legs becomes unbearable, slowly raise the posture, but do not stand up completely. The hips should always maintain a degree of relaxation. Then, when the pain finally disperses and strength has been regained, sink down once again to a low posture. Pay careful attention that the knees do not push outwards, fold inwards, or extend beyond the toes. The toes, heels, balls and sides of the feet should all make contact with the ground except for the *yongquan* point on the sole of the foot (in the center of the arch) which should be kept hollow.

In the beginning to intermediate stages of taiji practice, one needs a teacher to check the body's alignment and make the necessary corrections. It is common for a student to feel intense heat consuming his body when the teacher corrects his posture ("fixes his frame") or even occasionally when he does so himself. This is merely the qi flowing freely once again after having been obstructed, like dammed water after a hole has appeared in the wall. It is the result of the acupuncture channels' having been opened and the blockages of qi removed as the body's posture is allowed to become more natural. This sensation, which is actually quite pleasant, disperses after a time when the qi becomes balanced.

The time one spends on this exercise depends on the individual's standard. The first ten minutes are always the hardest. After this, time appears to pass at an increasing rate. Suddenly one day one may discover that forty minutes or even an hour has flown by.

ZHANZHUANG
How to Stand Like a Mountain

1) Stand naturally. Feet together. Hands at the sides. Hips slightly relaxed. The ears, shoulders, hips, knees, and ankles should all be in a straight line to maintain body balance (photos 1; 1a sideview). In this instance the musculature surrounding the dantian is not needed, so the dantian can relax and open which means that more qi will flow through it and be available to the rest of the body. The more qi which can return to the dantian from the internal organs, the more vitality one will have.
2) Close the mouth with the tongue resting lightly on the upper palate to facilitate the flow of qi downwards, and close the eyes (or if you prefer you can allow them to remain open).
3) Repeat the following words to yourself as a mental checklist: "Weight balance. Mind balance. Listening behind. Dantian qi balance."
4) Slowly bend the knees and relax the hips to lower the center of gravity and allow the qi to sink more.

5) Transfer the weight onto the right leg. Sink down. Lift the heel of the left foot and then the toes (photo 2). Step out to a position shoulder-width (with the weight still solid/firm on the right leg) placing the toes to the ground first and then the heel (photo 3), slowly shifting the weight to the center so that it is balanced between both legs (photo 4; 4a sideview). Do not transfer the weight as you step out. This leads to "double-weighting."

6) Again, repeat silently, "Weight balance. Mind balance. Listening behind. Dantian qi balance." Relax the spine from the neck down to the coccyx. As you mentally relax each vertebrae, count from one to nine. As the qi sinks the dantian becomes stronger and should feel very comfortable. Internally, the body becomes like the taiji image.
7) Very slowly rise the hands to a position shoulder height and shoulder width (photos 5, 6 and 6a). The arms can be slightly wider than the shoulders to open the chest and allow more qi to sink to the dantian. As the hands raise, simultaneously sink the hips more deeply and relax. It is imperative that the shoulders and elbows be relaxed and sunk and the wrists loose. In other words, do not fully extend the arms, straightening the elbows and fingers.
8) When the arms are at the correct position, repeat again "Mind balance. Weight balance. Listening behind. Dantian qi balance."

9) Now find the most comfortable position (i.e. check that the chest is concave, and shoulders and hips are as relaxed as possible). You may need to make slight adjustments if any part of the body feels stiff or tense. When you feel comfortable hold this position. Stand firm "like a mountain" for as long as possible (photos 7).
10) When you decide to finish the exercise, repeat again: "Mind balance. Weight balance. Listening behind. Dantian qi balance."
11) Very very slowly lower the hands down to the sides. At the same time stand up slowly, though not completely. The hips should still maintain a degree of relaxation (photo 5).

12) Repeat once more: "Mind balance. Weight balance. Listening behind. Dantian qi balance."
13) Slowly transfer the weight back to the right leg. Lift the heel and then the toes of the left foot and replace the left leg next to the right (photos 3 and 2). As the foot lands, plant the toes first and then the heel. The hips are still relaxed at this point.
14) For the very last time repeat the words: "Mind balance. Weight balance. Listening behind. Dantian qi balance." Count silently, one through nine.
15) Then slowly stand all the way up. The hips are now straight. You are back to the original position (photo 8).
16) Relax and slowly open the eyes. This completes standing pole or wuji standing. After cultivating stillness, one is ready to begin taiji movement. It is generally best to follow this exercise with silk-reeling exercises prior to forms practice.

SILK-REELING
Exercise #1 Single-Hand

This exercise requires the practitioner to work both left and right sides of the body. The number of times that silk is reeled should be equal on both sides. You can begin with ten times and go to fifty or more on each side. The eyes should focus lightly on the hand (the middle finger especially) and follow as it moves in wide circles. Technically the hand should not pass higher than the eyebrows or lower than the chin, though some teachers claim no higher than the top of the head or lower than the shoulders. The size of the circles described by the hand are directly related to the width of the stance.

Beginning with the left side first, the procedure for the opening position is as follows:

1) Stand naturally. Feet together. Hands by the sides. Relax the hips and bend the knees slightly (photo 1).
2) Place the right hand on the hip. Left hand by the side. The weight should be balanced between the legs (photo 2).
3) Bend the knees more deeply and sink down. Transfer the weight to the right leg. Lift the heel of the left foot followed by the toes (photo 3), and step out to the side in a wide stance landing with the heel first and then the toes. At the same time as the left leg steps out, turn the waist towards the right with the left hand following the waist, palm pushing to the right (without force) to a position above the knee and opposite the dantian (photo 4).

4) Relax the wrist and raise the hand to approximately shoulder height; turning the palm outwards (photos 5 and 6).

5) Transfer the weight to the left leg and turn the waist to the left. The left hand follows the waist and describes an arc, to a position shoulder-height but wider than the shoulders in front of the body (photos 7, 8, and 9). Relax the shoulder and keep the elbow sunk (lower than the shoulder), otherwise the shoulder will become tense and the qi will become blocked.

Without pausing, follow the proceeding steps:

Step 1: With weight on the left leg, drop the left elbow as the hand spirals inwards in a circular motion down to waist-height to the left of the hips, with the palm facing right (qi travels to the waist) (photo 10).

Step 2. Transfer the weight to the right leg and turn the waist to the right. The hand follows the waist to a position opposite the dantian above the right knee—as in opening movement (qi passes to the dantian) (photos 11 and 4).

Step 3. With the weight still on the right leg, relax the wrist and raise the arm to a position opposite the right shoulder, turning the palm outwards as in opening movement (qi travels up the back and to the shoulders) (photo 6).

Step 4. Transfer the weight to the left. At the same time, turn the waist and move the hand in a circular motion to a position outside of the left shoulder in front of the body-as in opening movement (qi passes through the arms to the fingertips) (photo 7). This completes one cycle. After Step 4 repeat the process 1 through 4 and continue on for a minimum of ten cycles each side to a maximum of fifty. To close on the left side follow the proceeding steps:

Step 5. On the last cycle follow steps 1, 2, and 3, and on the 4th step, as you turn the palm outwards and transfer the weight to the left leg, close the right leg by lifting the heel and then the toe and replacing the toe and then the heel next to the left foot. The weight is still sunk with the knees bent (photo 12).

Step 6. Raise the right hand until it comes to a position opposite the left hand, about shoulder height (photo 13).

Step 7. Lower both hands together down the center (fingers facing inwards) and straighten the legs at the same time (photo 14). The hands come back to a position at the sides of the thighs, as in the natural opening position (photo 1). To begin the right side, follow the preceding steps from the opening position to the closing position, but reverse all instructions so you have a mirror image. When you close the right side, this completes the single hand silk-reeling exercise.

SILK-REELING
Exercise #2 Double-Hand

This exercise also works both the left and right sides. Begin with the left.
1) Stand naturally with arms by the sides and feet together. The weight is balanced. The hips are relaxed and sunk, and the knees slightly bent (photo 1).
2) Pivot on the right heel and turn the right toes out at a ninety-degree angle (photo 2).
3) Bend the knees and sink down more. Transfer the weight to the right (rear) leg and lift the left heel. At the same time turn both palms to face the rear, waist height—the left hand is carried more forward, opposite the dantian, and the right hand is outside of the right hip (photos 3–4).

4) Lift the left toes and step forward into a deep stance at forty-five degrees, landing with the heel and then the toes. As you step, turn the waist to the rear; hands follow. The toes of the front leg are turned slightly inwards to maintain a line with the knee (photo 5). Twine hands clockwise to face the front (photos 6–7).
5) Transfer the weight to the left (front) leg (photo 8). Turn the waist to the left. The hands follow with the left hand parallel to the left knee and the right hand opposite the dantian (photo 9). The left hand is carried naturally slightly higher than the right. This is the opening position. Throughout the proceeding cycles the eyes follow the hands.

Step 1. Weight on the left leg. Relax the wrists and raise the arms together turning the palms to face outwards, hands approximately shoulder height, elbows sunk and shoulders relaxed (left hand, qi to the waist; right hand, qi to the back) (photos 10–11).

Step 2. Transfer the weight to the rear (right leg) and turn the waist to the right with the hands following. The left hand comes to a position opposite the left shoulder with the right hand carried outside to the rear with both palms facing outwards (left hand, qi to the dantian; right hand, qi to the fingers) (photos 12-13).

Step 3. While keeping the weight on the right, move the arms downwards in an arc to a position waist height. The left hand is in front of the right hip, palm facing downwards, and the right hand is carried to the rear, outside of the right hip and palm facing slightly forward (left hand, qi to the back; right hand, qi to the waist) (photo 5).

Step 4. Transfer the weight to the front (left leg). Turn the waist to the left and front with the hands following, left hand in front of the left hip and right hand in front of the dantian (left hand, qi to the fingers; right hand, qi to the dantian) (photos 6-9).

This is one complete cycle. Repeat as many times as you feel comfortable, being sure to balance the number of repetitions on both sides.

When you decide to finish the left side and begin the right, on the last cycle follow steps 1, 2, 3, and on the 4th step, as you transfer the weight to the front (left leg) and the hands follow the waist to the dantian, close the right leg next to the left (photo 14).

In a closing position raise the arms in an arc to shoulder height (photos 15–16) then lower them down the center to the sides and straighten the legs, returning to the natural beginning position (photo 1).

To work silk-reeling on the opposite side, follow the instructions above but reverse the instructions, i.e. begin with turning the left toes out at a ninety-degree angle and step out with the right foot, etc. Reverse the directions for steps 1 through 4. Close in the same manner as before.

With both of these exercises don't step too wide. Chen stylists are noted for their low stances but these should not be forced. You have to know yourself, your strength, body structure, and range of motion. Then you can determine the width of your stance, how low you can sit, and which posture is right for you. The general rule is to be natural. Otherwise the qi will not flow freely and your movement will be restricted.

All silk-reeling exercises should be performed in a very relaxed and comfortable manner. A common mistake is to use too much energy or force. In this case the arms will become stiff. The movements should be slow, fluid and continuous, without interruption. Through both standing pole and silk-reeling the mass of the practitioner's thighs increases dramatically, making his gait stronger and steadier. The sinking and rooting achieved through these skills opens the hips and increases the mobility of the waist, necessary in neutralizing an opponent's energy. There are no mystical powers in taiji. The seemingly impossible, or "super-human" ability to throw an opponent twelve feet away, is all accomplished through correct *gongfu* (time and energy spent) and understanding and applying the taiji principles.

Most real confrontations on the street are concluded on the ground with both parties struggling for control through wrestling and grappling. The winner is invariably the stronger person. However, one who is well trained in standing pole is extremely hard to push as his root is so strong (through relaxed sinking, not the use of raw muscle power). He is, therefore, master of his own balance and can dissolve the greatest force from any direction because his waist is like an axle, having been forged through the training of silk-reeling. Without silk-reeling, the spiraling necessary for advanced qinna techniques (the ability to follow the opponent as he attempts to escape or to escape from them oneself) and body strikes are extremely difficult to accomplish. Ren Guangyi is quick to point out that one can learn qinna without learning taiji silk-reeling, but his level will not be as high. Qinna is not applied using force against force, but with "listening skill" combined with good technique and coordinated waist power.

Push-hands: Chen Xiaowang and Ren Guangyi demonstrating.

To apply qinna one must be very quick, using the element of surprise by feinting one direction and then switching or following the opponent. The latter requires sensitivity to know in which direction the enemy is heading and to beat him there. Also to escape qinna requires one first to relax and sink the hips, in other words to be rooted, and then to use the subtle coiling motion developed through intensive silk-reeling training. The internal energy travels and changes in the chest and waist, and passes through the shoulders and elbows; when the strength has reached the wrist, one can escape. Only when the shoulders and elbow joints are clear and unobstructed can the internal energy reach the fingers. The shoulders connect with the hips (the elbows with the knees and the hands with the feet), so unless the hips can relax, the shoulders will be stiff. It is extremely difficult, if not impossible, to escape qinna once one's feet have already been lifted off the ground by a painful joint lock, or after one has already been forced to the floor.

The object of standing, silk-reeling, and form practice is to achieve balance, fifty percent hard and fifty percent soft, yin and yang. In this situation Man and Nature become One. Generally, in push-hands people are naturally tense, so yang (hardness) comes more easy to them than yin (softness). When one uses physical strength the tendency is to strain and become stiff. In this case it is very difficult to attain softness through relaxation when it is needed. Therefore, this should be the primary intention when practicing foundation training. On the other hand, if one has attained relaxation and softness, one can achieve hardness at will and there will be more internal strength at ones disposal.

To reach a high level of taijiquan, repetitive daily practice of bare-handed forms is, of course, imperative. But many practitioners only concentrate on these and disregard the foundations. If the ability to perform the taiji forms spontaneously in demonstration and the ability to apply them in a free-style manner in real life situations (the purpose for which they were designed) is the fluent language of the art, and the forms (routine training) contain the vocabulary and sentences, then the practice of standing pole and silk-reeling provides the sounds upon which the language is based. They cannot be disregarded.

Pinyin	Wade-Giles	Chinese
bafa	pa fa	八法
bagua	pakua	八卦
bai hui	pai hui	百會
chansijing	ch'an szu ching	纏蘇經
Chenjiagou	Ch'en chia kou	陳家溝
cunjing	ts'un ching	寸勁
dantian	tan t'ien	丹田
dao	tao	道
daoyin	tao yin	導引
erlu	erh lu	二路
fajing	fa ching	發勁
gongfu	kung fu	功夫
gua	kua	卦
Henan	Honan	河南
huiyin	huiyin	會陰
jingluo	ching lo	經絡
jingmai	ching mai	經脈
lanzhayi	lan cha i	懶扎衣
laojia	laochia	老架
ming men	ming men	命門
Paochui	P'ao ch'ui	炮捶
qi	ch'i	氣
qigong	ch'i kung	氣功
qinna	ch'in na	擒拿
Shaolin	Shaolin	少林
taiji	t'ai chi	太極
taijiquan	t'ai chi ch'üan	太極拳
tingjing	t'ing ching	聽勁
tuishou	t'ui shou	推手
wuji	wu chi	無極
xinjia	hsin chia	新架
xingyi	hsing i	形意
Yijing	*I-ch'ing*	易經
yilu	i lu	一路
yongquan	yong ch'üan	涌泉
zhanzhuang	chan chuang	站樁

Pinyin	Wade-Giles	Chinese
Chen Fake	Ch'en Fa-k'o	陳發科
Chen Zhangxing	Ch'en Chang-hsing	陳長興
Chen Wangting	Chen Wang-t'ing	陳王廷
Chen Qingping	Ch'en Ch'ing-p'ing	陳青萍
Chen Xiaowang	Ch'en Hsiao-wang	陳小旺
Li Bantian	Li Pan-t'ien	李半天
Qi Jiguang	Ch'i Chi-kuang	戚繼光
Ren Guangyi	Jen Kuang-i	任廣義
Sun Lutang	Sun Lutang	孫祿堂
Tang Hao	T'ang Hao	唐豪
Wu Jianquan	Wu Chien-ch'uan	武鑒泉
Yang Chengfu	Yang Ch'eng-fu	楊橙甫
Yang Luchan	Yang Lu-ch'an	楊露禪
Zhang Bojing	Chang Po-ching	張伯敬

References

Berwick, S. (1997, October). The five stages of Chen combat training. *Inside Kung Fu,* 106–111.

Berwick, S. (1997, October). Chen combat training. *Inside Kung Fu,* 106–111.

Berwick, S. (1997, December-January). Chen combat. *WushuKung Fu,* 23–25; 40–41.

Bissell, G. (1993, February). Chen style taiji changquan and the five routines of taijiquan. *The Journal of the Chen Style Taijiquan Research Association of Hawaii, 1*(1), 7–9.

Chen, X. The lectures and teachings of Chen Xiaowang: New York seminars July 20–21, 1996, and September 27–28, 1997, sponsored by Ren Guangyi; Rutherford, New Jersey, Mountain View Martial Arts, April 22, 1996, and September 30, 1997, sponsored by Greg Pinney.

Chi, J. (1993, October). Training techniques for Chen style skills. *Tai Chi, 17*(6), 8–11.

Gu, L. (1984). The origin, evolution and development of shadow boxing. In Zhaohua Publishing House (compilers), *Chen style taijiquan* (pp. 1–12). Hong Kong: Hai Feng Publishing Company.

Kuo, L. (1994). *The t'ai chi boxing chronicle* (Guttman, Trans.). Berkeley, CA: North Atlantic Books.

Liang, B. (1993, August). Sparring techniques in Chen style. *The Journal of the Chen Style Taijiquan Research Association of Hawaii, 1*(4), 1–3.

Ren, G. Personal instruction from Ren Guangyi, New York, 1992 to 1997.

Tse, M. (1994, June). Wuji and taiji. *Combat,* 80–81.

Tse, M. (1995, January). The martial art of Chen Wangting. *Combat,* 74–75.

An Introduction to Seizing Techniques in Chen Style Taijiquan

by Yaron Seidman, L.Ac.

All photographs by Thomas Yeong.

Introduction

Chen taijiquan is the oldest of the taiji schools, dating back to the seventeenth century. This martial arts style is known for developing the fighting skills of its practitioners on various levels. The first and most basic skill is dealing with an incoming attack at the physical level. At this level, the practitioner learns to relax and adjust his body to the incoming power. By doing that, the attack is dissolved and the practitioner changes his defense into attack. While at this phase, it is common to use seizing techniques. The practitioner locks his opponent's joints, thus ending the fight.

Qinna translates from Chinese Mandarin as "seizing and catching," however, it also means catching and putting somebody in a difficult position. It is an inseparable part of every Chinese martial artist's curriculum. Chen taijiquan is no different. As a martial art based on the principles of taiji and the so-called "thirteen postures," taijiquan utilizes qinna application within its frame of concept. The "thirteen postures" are thirteen arts of energy:

meet	follow
push	press
pluck	adverse
elbow	lean
advance	retreat
rightwards	leftwards
centering	

These energy arts are closely integrated in qinna techniques. Examples can be found on the following pages: "meeting" (A1), "following" (B4), "pressing" (E4).

In reality, every single technique contains the whole thirteen postures. While applying qinna, the whole body is reacting as a one unified life energy (*qi*), which means that every part of the body is synchronizing with all other parts to work as one force. In one single technique, it is sometimes necessary for the hands to meet, the legs to follow, the anatomical center (*dantian*) to press, and the elbows to adverse all at the same time.

The taiji principle is "yin and yang." Yin and yang is "softness and hardness" and "slow and quick." In taijiquan's qinna techniques, the practitioner must clearly distinguish hardness and softness and moving slowly and quickly. When the opponent is hard, one must be very soft and follow. When the opponent yields, one must be very hard and penetrating. When the opponent is moving slowly, one must follow slowly and adhere. When the opponent is moving fast, one must respond quickly and reach first. As it is clearly stated in the taiji classics: "When you do not move, I do not move. When you move, I move first. When the opponent's internal energy reaches my skin, my internal energy reaches his bone marrow".

Keeping that in mind, the practitioner is primarily practicing taijiquan, as well as using qinna to supplement it. There are many steps on the path to mastering the vast field of taijiquan. Qinna is a building block on this path, which every practitioner should encounter and get familiar with.

TECHNICAL SECTION
Techniques demonstrated by Chen Zhonghua and Yaron Seidman.

1) WRIST LOCK — as in the form Buddha's Warrior Pounds the Mortar.
  1a) Starting in the initial position for practicing all the different locking techniques (1 thru 5), two people face each other while standing about six feet apart.
  1b) When the attacker steps in and punches with his right fist, the defender steps in immediately with his right hand meeting the right wrist and his left hand meeting the attacker's right elbow.
  1c) The defender then pushes his right hand forward, causing the punching hand to bend backwards toward the attacker's face. At the same time, the defender's left hand controls the attacker's right elbow from moving. At this stage, it is important for the defender to have both his elbows close to each other to gain control over the attacker's arm.
  1d) The defender sinks and uses his body weight to press down on the attacker's right wrist. At the same time, the defender uses his left hand to push the attacker's right elbow upward.
  1e) The defender turns his waist towards the left and sinks more, bringing the attacker down to the ground.

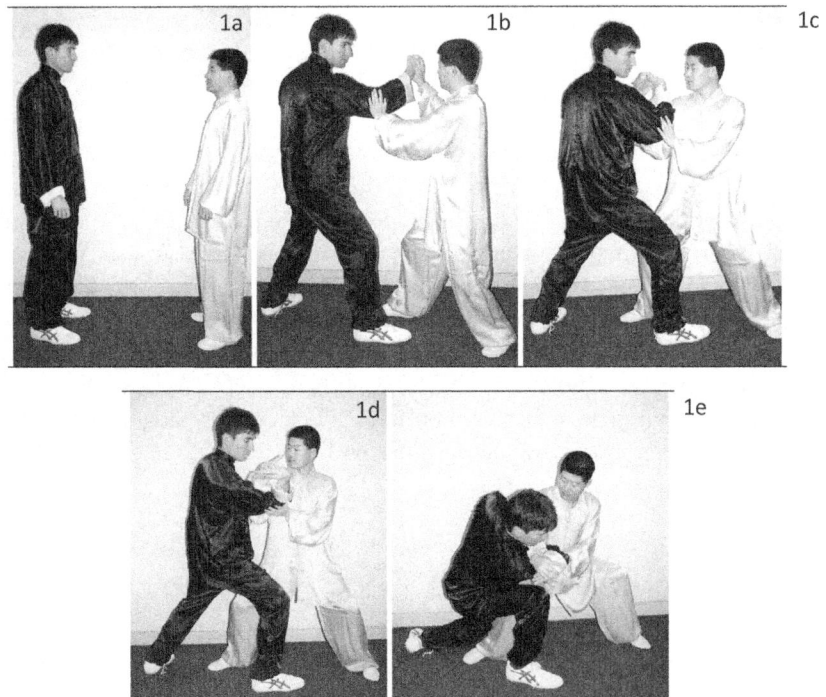

Points of attention:
In this technique, it is vital to synchronize the movements of the hands with the movements of the hips and legs. In addition, when pulling the opponent down, it is mandatory to keep oneself in an upright position, and not bend forward.

2) ELBOW LOCK — as in Six Sealing and Four Closing.
- **2a)** When the attacker steps in and punches with his left fist, the defender meets the attacker's left wrist with his left hand.
- **2b)** The defender continues to advance with his right foot and places his right wrist on the attacker's left elbow.
- **2c)** The defender then uses his left hand to pull the attacker's left fist downward. At the same time, he presses with his right palm on the attacker's elbow.
- **2d)** The defender then bends his right knee and presses down with his right forearm on the attacker's elbow while using his left hand to pull the attacker's forearm backward and upward.
- **2e)** Following this last move, the defender can shift his weight on to the left foot, using the momentum to pull the attacker off his feet.

Points of attention:
The defender's right elbow must synchronize well with his left hand. Pulling, grabbing and twisting all must happen together. In addition when shifting the weight onto the left foot, the right foot must keep rooted into the ground. The posture must stay upright and not lean forward or sideways.

3) SHOULDER LOCK — as in Part the Horses Mane.
- **3a)** When the attacker steps in and punches with his left fist, the defender takes a small step with his right foot and blocks the attack with his left hand.
- **3b)** Immediately after that, the defender steps in with his right foot, placing his right arm underneath the attacker's left upper arm.
- **3c)** He then pushes the attacker's left hand downward and his upper arm upward, so that the attacker's left shoulder and elbow are locked.
- **3d)** The defender then sinks and turns his waist to the right, pressing with his right elbow on the attacker's left ribs, causing him to lose balance.

Points of attention:
While locking the attacker's shoulder and lifting him up, the defender must keep his feet rooted to the ground.

4) HIP LOCK — as in Turn the Flowers Out of the Bottom of the Sea.
  4a) When the attacker steps in to strike with his left fist, the defender immediately steps in and uses his left hand to block the attack.
  4b) The defender steps behind the attacker's left foot and, at the same time, inserts his right forearm under the attacker's left upper arm.
  4c) The defender then moves his arm upward and his left hand downward which locks the attacker's left elbow while breaking the rooting of his right foot.
  4d) The defender then turns his hips to the right, raises his right knee pushing the attacker's left knee upward. At the same time, the defender presses down with his right elbow on the left side of the attacker's ribcage, causing him to lose his balance and fall backward.

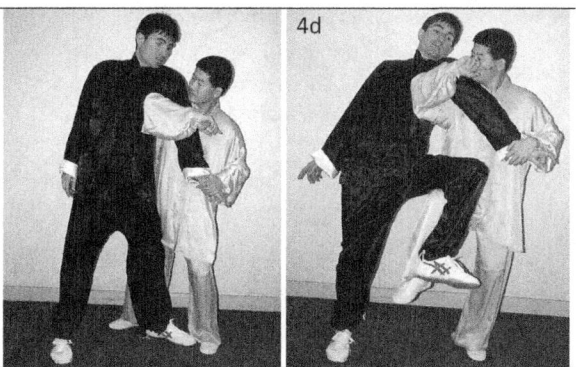

Points of attention:
In this technique, prior to locking the attacker's hip, it is necessary to lock his left elbow and sever his right foot rooting. This action causes the attacker to rely on his left foot for balance. As a result, when the defender raises his right knee, pushing the attacker's left knee upward, the attacker will lose balance and fall down.

5) WHOLE BODY LOCK — as in the form Wade Forward and Twist Step.

5a) When the attacker steps in with his right foot, using his right hand to grasp the defender's right hand, the defender immediately steps in with his right foot, and offers slight resistance to the grab.

5b) The defender then places his left hand on top of the attacker's right hand. The defender holds the attacker's right hand to his own wrist, eliminating the possibility of the attacker escaping. The defender pushes his right hand upward, turns his hips and right hand to the right, locking the attacker's right elbow and shoulder.

5c) Without pausing, the defender sinks his waist down, pushing the attacker's right forearm down, further locking the attacker's right hip.

5d) The defender then pushes his own anatomical center (*dantian*) forward and downward, locking the attacker's right knee as well.

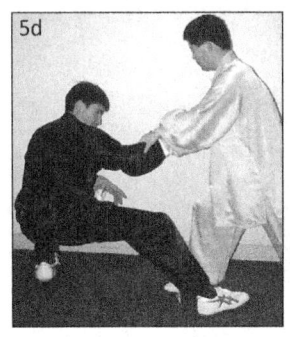

Points for attention:
In this technique, it is important to synchronize the movements of the defender's right hand and hips. At a beginner level, it is necessary for the defender to use both his hands to lock the attacker's joints (as demonstrated above). However, at a more advanced level, the defender will use only his right hand to lock the attacker's whole body.

Conclusion

Taijiquan combat skills have several levels. The most basic one is using the muscles and joints to deal with an opponent. At a higher level, it is important to sense the opponent's energy and neutralize it with one's own energy. The highest skill is to know the opponent's intentions before they are initiated.

When learning taijiquan, the levels of progress are: 1) training the body (as in qinna techniques); 2) training the energy (*qi*); and 3) at the highest realm, training the mind/intentions (*yi*). However, knowledge of body mechanics and qinna are essential for ones progress and cannot be overlooked.

Three Techniques of Dantian Rotation in Chen Taiji: Internal Energy Techniques and Their Relationship with the Body's Meridians

by Bosco Seung-Chul Baek (白承哲), B.S.

Photography and graphics by Chris Soule.

Introduction

Chen family taijiquan is the original system from which all other taiji styles are ultimately derived. The ninth-generation representative, Chen Wangting (1580–1660), created taijiquan from boxing heritages of past generations. Unlike other taijiquan styles, the Chen style still utilizes explosive power (*fajing*), as expressed in the practice routine called "cannon fist." Authentic taijiquan requires harmony of four characteristics: sturdiness, softness, fastness, and slowness. It is impossible to master Chen taiji without these characteristics. To become relaxed and grounded, exercises and routines are practiced slowly, including the old frame first routine, since it helps one to deeply relax the muscles, joints, and spine while breathing naturally.

Training with speed, such as in the old frame second routine, helps a practitioner understand the use of the fast energy exchange between the positive and negative forces within the body and thus increase the power from one's *dantian*, which is the physical center of balance and energy. If a practitioner trains under a qualified Chen-style instructor, he or she should be able to get familiar with the dantian and learn to internally control its rotational movements (*neizhuan*) and utilize its function as a source of movement and power.

Before attempting any complex practice, it is a prerequisite to open one's energy pathways so that the dantian circulates qi powerfully. In other words, anywhere energy is blocked in the body should be unblocked by circulating energy (*qi*) through the energy meridians. For instance, if a practitioner has an injury or ailment, qi will not flow smoothly through that impaired area. However, the practitioner may remove foul energy caused by the ailment by silk-reeling practice to circulate qi through the area.

Silk-reeling is defined as a spiral movement that initiates from the dantian and leads the rest of one's body movement. All taiji movements must originate from the dantian to be done properly—this is the key concept in the silk-reeling method. In order to circulate and cultivate powerful energy by silk-reeling practice, one should know how to mentally direct energy flow through certain internal pathways. These pathways, called meridians, circulate energy throughout the body. A correct understanding of the meridians helps one to direct energy through the meridians naturally. With time and practice, the relationship between taijiquan and the meridian system will become progressively closer.

In order to maximize the use of meridians, it is important to acquire certain techniques of dantian internal rotation. In Chen taijiquan, silk-reeling energy is activated due to these dantian rotations, and with consistent practice, it eventually interpenetrates through the meridians. The following descriptions are authentic training methods of Chen taijiquan's silk-reeling and dantian internal rotations.

Silk-Reeling Energy

Silk-reeling is the key practice in Chen taiji that focuses on moving spiral energy from the dantian throughout the entire body. When the dantian rotates, all related joints and muscles follow its direction. From a dantian's movement, silk-reeling energy will penetrate through the hips, knees, ankles, waist, back, shoulders, elbows, wrists, and fingertips. In this way, a practitioner can circulate qi through the entire body and sink energy into the dantian area. Eventually, a practitioner can learn to harmonize energy between the body and mind by stimulating meridian energy pathways. After becoming familiar with the basic silk-reeling exercises, practicing the old frame first routine instills profound knowledge of the various expressions of silk-reeling energy found within its different postures. If the basic silk-reeling practice is not deep, old frame practice will fail to embody the guiding principles of the art.

Understanding the Eight Extraordinary Meridians

To circulate energy effectively, it is important to know basic meridian pathways for silk-reeling exercises. It is believed that Chen Wangting created taijiquan by synthesizing yin-yang theory and breathing exercises that nourish qi (*daoyin tuna*) with twenty-nine postures found in General Qi Jiguang's (1528–1588) book on military tactics (*New Book Recording Effective Techniques*), and Chinese medical meridian theory. Understanding how meridians function is important for making progress with silk-reeling exercises, breathing exercises, and related forms of inner cultivation.

It is easy to observe that many taijiquan practitioners lack knowledge of meridians theory. Any practice without this understanding would not seize the essence of taijiquan and could easily become a "taiji-like dance." Chen taijiquan aims to involve the use of meridians through the practice of standing post (*zhanzhuang*), silk-reeling exercises, and the practice routines. Without these progressive steps, it is inauthentic. During this process hands-on correction from a teacher is mandatory to acquire genuine taijiquan skills.

In Chinese medicine, the eight extraordinary meridians are considered the root of energy pathways, while the twelve standard meridians would be considered branches. Even more sophisticated meridians cannot exist without the eight extraordinary and twelve standard meridians. The terms "vessel" and "course" are also commonly used to denote an energy pathway. Diagrams are included below for reference, showing only the main meridians from the complete list of eight extraordinary and twelve standard meridians. For more detailed information, please refer to meridian diagrams in Chinese medical textbooks.

The most important meridians in the body are called the eight extraordinary meridians, which we will discuss in the following paragraphs:

1) directing   3) penetrating   5) yin linking   7) yin heel
2) governing   4) girdle   6) yang linking 8) yang heel

Simplified Diagrams of Four Extraordinary Meridians

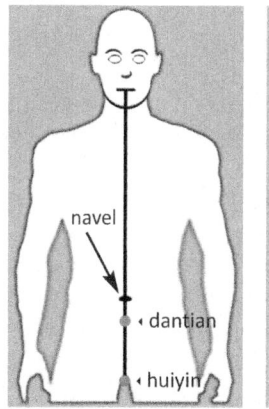
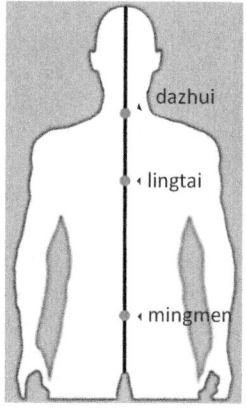

Left, directing meridian: *Dantian* exists approximately 1.79 inches below the navel. *Huiyin* is the perineum. **Right, governing meridian:** *Mingmen* exists between lumbar 2 and lumbar 3 on the spinal column. *Lingtai* exists at thoracic 6 on the spinal column. *Dazhui* exists at cervical 7 on the spinal column.

Simplified Diagrams of
Four Extraordinary Meridians

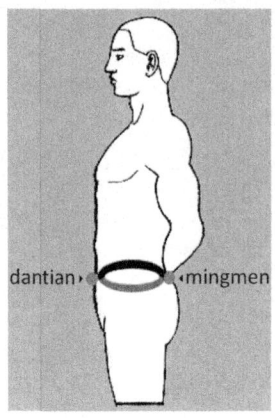

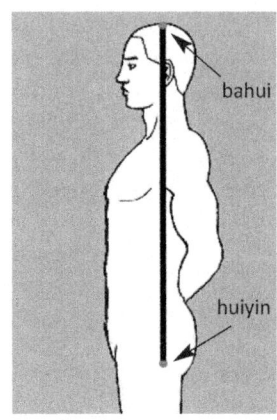

Left, girdle meridian: *Dantian* exists approximately 1.79 inches below the navel. *Mingmen* exists between lumbar 2 and lumbar 3 on the spinal column.
Right, penetrating meridian (back): *Huiyin* is the perineum. *Baihui* is 8.33 inches above the midpoint of the posterior hairline and 5.95 inches above the midpoint of the anterior hairline.

Extraordinary meridians are powerfully independent regardless of the sequence of energy circulation in the pathways. For example, it is possible to activate the girdle vessel before the meridians in the legs and still maximize the effectiveness of each meridian. In other words, it is possible to take advantage of part of these extraordinary meridians individually or in unison. This is why they are considered extraordinary. However, the goal is to synchronize these meridians. If there is a blockage due to an ailment, the meridians cannot be combined. In order to lessen this type of error, Chen taijiquan aims to develop four extraordinary meridians in the lower body at the start of training. These are located in the calcaneus (heel bone: the yang heel and yin heel vessels) and in the talus (ankle bone: the yang linking and yin linking vessels).

The standing post and silk-reeling practices both vigorously stimulate the four extraordinary meridians that pass through the legs due to the dantian's central place in these exercises and the effects of gravity on the thighs. It is not necessary to make an effort to sense the energy in these meridians because it brings a very physical and direct stimulation of the legs. This is the reason the four meridians in the lower body are omitted in the aforementioned diagram of the eight extraordinary meridians. For instance, the thighs feel burning and shaking because the upper body's energy is condensed into the dantian, and the lower body makes full spiraling movements when executing silk-reeling movements. The hip, knee, ankle, and all related muscles, joints, and nerves are used to make the spiraling and coiling movements from the dantian internal rotations, which produce silk-reeling energy. These meridians are linked throughout the entire body. Unless the meridians are fully opened, there is normally physical pain while practicing, but this is how a practitioner is able to dissipate any blockage in the meridians. A few indications of powerful energy cultivation and dissipating a blockage in the meridians are a burning sensation in the thighs, shaking legs, and warmness throughout the body.

The girdle vessel is directly related to opening the dantian because its meridian pathway passes through the lower abdominals and the waist area. In other words, it controls the internal organs that exist in the lower abdominal area. There is a specific technique to use this meridian in Chen taijiquan. The key is conditioning the upper body and lumbar to allow a practitioner to breathe naturally. In this way, a practitioner is able to activate the girdle vessel by natural breathing. This specific technique requires physical movements of the lower abdominal muscles and lumbar with inhalation and exhalation. In order to execute this, the dantian and mingmen should have horizontal alignment to be stabilized. The technique for the girdle vessel will be explained later in this article.

The penetrating vessel is considered the most difficult energy pathway to acquire because it passes through an internal spinal course. If the seven vessels of the eight extraordinary meridians are truly open, then it satisfies a prerequisite to train this vessel. The use of this vessel should only be taught after clearly mastering the "small heavenly circle" and the "big heavenly circle" (established when the directing and governing vessels are connected). A master can test a student's success in circulating energy through these pathways by confirming it through subtly sensing it with his own hands.

Direct lineage masters and grandmasters of Chen taijiquan—such as Chen Xiaowang, Chen Xiaoxing, Chen Yu, and Chen Bing—still possess all dantian internal-rotation techniques for opening all of the eight extraordinary and twelve standard meridians. This instruction is only open to their disciples.

Understanding the Twelve Standard Meridians

In addition to the eight extraordinary meridians, there are the twelve standard meridians that are directly derived from internal organs. For silk-reeling and dantian-rotation practices, only three of the standard meridians are usually used with two of the eight extraordinary meridians. Therefore, nine of the twelve standard meridians are omitted for simplification.

The Twelve Standard Meridians
- lung meridian of the hand (*taiyin*)
- heart meridian of the hand (*shaoyin*)
- pericardium meridian of the hand (*jueyin*)
- sanjiao meridian of the hand (*shaoyang*)
- small-intestine meridian of the hand (*taiyang*)
- large-intestine meridian of the hand (*yangming*)
- spleen meridian of the foot (*taiyin*)
- kidney meridian of the foot (*shaoyin*)
- liver meridian of the foot (*jueyin*)
- gallbladder meridian of the foot (*shaoyang*)
- bladder meridian of the foot (*taiyang*)
- stomach meridian of the foot (*yangming*)

The Three Standard Meridians
- pericardium meridian of the hand (*jueyin*)
- spleen meridian of the foot (*taiyin*)
- small-intestine meridian of the hand (*taiyang*)

The Two Extraordinary Meridians
- directing
- governing

jing luo

經絡

    Since the eight extraordinary meridians are the true source of all energy pathways, it is not required to use all of the twelve meridians for dantian-rotation exercises. In silk-reeling exercises, the directing and governing vessels are combined because together they synergistically employ the eight extraordinary and twelve standard meridians at the same time. The primary meridians utilized in practice are the pericardium meridian of the hand, the spleen meridian of the foot, and the small-intestine meridian of the hand.

Simplified Diagrams of Three Standard Meridians

Pericardium Meridian of the Hand
- *Zhongchong* is in the center of the middle finger.
- *Laogong* is between the second and third metacarpal bones.
- *Quze* is at the ulnar side of the biceps brachii tendon.
- *Tianchi* is about 1.19 inches lateral to the nipple in the fourth intercostal space.

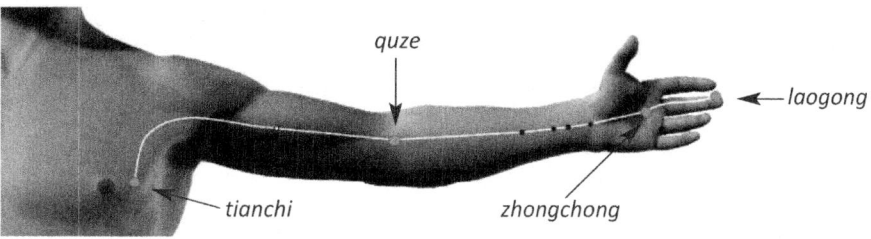

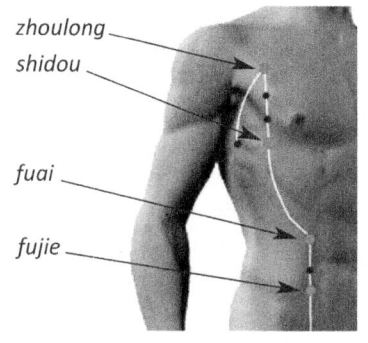

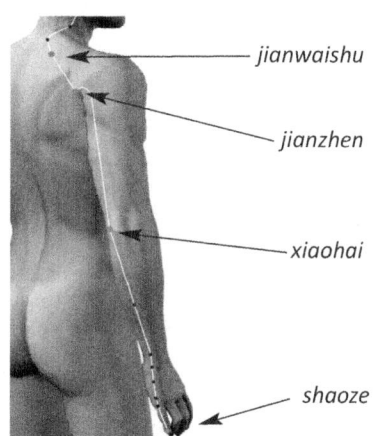

Left: Spleen Meridian of the Foot
- *Zhourong* is 7.14 inches lateral to the anterior midline in the second intercostal space.
- *Shidou* is 7.14 inches lateral to the anterior midline in the fifth intercostal space.
- *Fuai* is 4.76 inches lateral to the anterior midline at the directing vessel.
- *Fujie* is 4.76 inches lateral to the anterior midline, on the lateral side of the rectus abdominal muscle.

Right: Small-Intestine Meridian of the Hand
- *Jianwaishu* is 3.57 inches lateral to the lower border of the spinal column of T1.
- *Jianzhen* is 1.19 inches above the posterior and inferior to the shoulder joint.
- *Xiaohai* is in a depression between the elbow and the ulna with elbow flexion.
- *Shaoze* is 0.119 inch posterior to the corner of the nail on the ulnar side of the little finger.

In the actual silk-reeling practice, two extraordinary meridians (the directing and governing vessels) are used with three standard meridians (the pericardium, spleen, and small-intestine vessels). Practitioners should become acquainted with the following guide, which provides an order for circulating energy in the meridians by visualizing the flow from point to point:

1) **Meridians:** Pericardium Meridian of the Hand + Spleen Meridian of the Foot
   Points: zhongchong ▸ laogong ▸ quze ▸ tianchi ▸ zhourong ▸ shidou ▸ fuai ▸ fujie

2) **Meridians:** Spleen Meridian of the Foot + Directing Meridian
   Points: fujie ▸ dantian

3) **Meridians:** Directing + Governing Meridians
   Points: huiyin ▸ mingmen ▸ lingtai ▸ dazhui

4) **Meridians:** Governing Meridian + the Small-Intestine Meridian of the Hand
   Points: dazhui ▸ jianwaishu ▸ jianzhen ▸ xiaohai ▸ shaoze

Whenever practicing silk-reeling exercises, one should visualize the progressive energy flow from point to point as outlined above. The intention must be very natural. If the level is unnatural and creates too much tension in the body, it is hard to maintain correct postures and circulate energy. The feeling should be maintained midway between consciousness and unconsciousness. If this kind of mental awareness can be maintained, it will open the energy pathways even if a practitioner has a serious ailment. All he or she needs is a strong desire and determined effort for regular practice.

Locating the Dantian

In order to maximize use of the meridians in the legs, it is necessary to know where the dantian exists and to learn what is known as "abdominal breathing." Generally speaking, the dantian is located three fingers downward from the navel, or approximately 1.79 inches below the navel. Since the dantian location varies due to different body shapes, this will vary slightly for each practitioner.

If you are not clear in understanding the concept, it is fine to think of the dantian as the central area of lower abdominals that controls the whole body. However, it is not just a muscular group or singular body part. It is like an antenna that senses and is connected to all of the big and small changes in the body. For instance, the dantian will feel uncomfortable and imbalanced if a practitioner has a physical error in body alignment or if the energy is not sunken. On the contrary, it will feel full and a sensation of heaviness is apparent, and should be very relaxed during silk-reeling exercises, or during any taijiquan practice for that matter. Additionally, the mind is able to be clear, calm, and peaceful. There should be a deep sense of stability and sensitivity in the dantian at all times during practice.

Opening the Dantian

In classical Chen taijiquan practice, one's quality of motion and use of internal energy is dependent upon the dantian. At a beginner's level, it is not easy to sense or feel the existence of the dantian because the body and mind are not yet experienced in taijiquan's fundamentals. There is a methodical way to open one's dantian, and this specific training method is called the standing post (*zhanzhuang*). To practice, the entire spine should be relaxed and a practitioner must utilize all of the taijiquan principles to sink energy into the dantian. Since taijiquan's principles are very well known, let us focus on specific techniques used to open one's dantian.

The first principle is to have the upper chest relaxed with a sunken diaphragm, while keeping the upper back slightly rounded. There is a common misunderstanding about this, as a lot of practitioners create tension in the upper body by making the upper chest too hollow. This and all other requirements should be done naturally. The second principle is to have the lower back (lumbar) relaxed so there is no convex or concave shape to it. If done correctly, the coccyx will be naturally rolled up so that a practitioner feels a physical expansion from the lumbar to the coccyx. With the chin in proper position and the neck muscles relaxed, a practitioner is able to expand the entire spine to sense it as "one big stick."

If the spine is truly relaxed, the energy point called *mingmen* will be ready to cultivate powerful energy. Mingmen is translated as the "door of life." The mingmen is located at the spine's protuberance between lumbar 2 and 3. In a correct standing post posture, a horizontal line can be visualized between the dantian and mingmen, which interpenetrate each other energetically. It is the main energy spot used for refreshing the entire spine while training in standing post and is the key practice to making the internal alchemy of taijiquan.

This horizontal alignment line of the dantian and mingmen is called *damai*, which is noted as the girdle meridian and activates the dantian (Note: This meridian is quite different from Chinese medicine's girdle meridian). It is important that this alignment be kept at all times during taijiquan practice because within these two energy points is where the dantian exists. Opening the girdle vessel is the seed to making the dantian truly open. In order to stimulate the dantian to be active, it is necessary to visualize breathing through it and the mingmen while in the standing post posture. The dantian and mingmen points expand naturally while inhaling, as a balloon is expanded when air is inserted in it. They contract while exhaling. Without proper instruction, there are health risks with this practice. It is important that a practitioner be taken care of by an authentic instructor with hands-on corrections. A clear sign of this technique done properly is warmness in the lower abdominals. A sensation of coldness in the dantian area is an indication of improper practice.

The mind's intention during this breathing practice has to be natural while still physically engaging the lower abdominals and back—ultimately executed with the same intent used in combative applications. Done properly, one should experience expansion and contraction of both the front and back of the waist while breathing. In this way, a practitioner will develop the dantian core and cultivate powerful energy with standing post practice. This is the stage of energy cultivation called "dantian breathing." In later stages of practice, the dantian and the mingmen should expand and retract by themselves. Delicate instruction from qualified instructors to properly learn this process of breathing is a necessity. If not, side effects may occur due to incorrect instruction or relaxation technique.

THREE TECHNIQUES OF DANTIAN INTERNAL ROTATION

After accomplishing the previous requirements of energy cultivation, it is important to contemplate how to circulate energy by silk-reeling from the dantian. According to the theory of dantian internal rotation, the dantian articulates in three-dimensional movements congruent with taijiquan's fundamental principles and requirements, such as "sink energy to the dantian," "loosen the waist," and "maintain a dantian base."

Standing-post practice cultivates energy in the dantian through the girdle meridian (*damai*). In a common standing posture, the dantian is blocked because it and the mingmen are not facing each other on a parallel line. Unlike Chinese medicine's meridians around the skin, the damai line in taijiquan internally penetrates directly through the dantian. This interpenetrating line required by standing post practice does not access the dantian for internal rotation, but if the dantian moves, there is silk-reeling energy. If the dantian does not initiate and control movement in the body, there will be no silk-reeling energy. The three physical techniques of dantian rotation consist of horizontal, vertical, and multidirectional internal rotations. Without this understanding, any form practice will be a dance-like taiji performance and will be ineffective in application.

FIRST TECHNIQUE: Horizontal Dantian Rotation
For a novice, the first technique is easy to sense and acquire because it only moves horizontally in two directions, to the left or the right. Building upon the principles of standing post practice, a practitioner now has to rotate the dantian horizontally. Practiced to the front, this silk-reeling exercise is designed to familiarize the horizontal dantian internal rotation.

Preparation: standing with feet together (Fig. 1)
This is not just a boring stationary position. It requires relaxing the whole body from head to toe. Wait until everything becomes calm and breathe deeply three or five times for deep relaxation. Do not start to practice unless you feel relaxed enough. When one is truly relaxed (*fangsong*), the body feels like jelly or pudding. It is a good sign to have a higher level of relaxation.

STEP 1: Lowering the Hand (Figs. 1a–b)
Slowly bring down the hand with the intention of activating meridians 1 and 2. To effectively lead the energy, focusing on the thumb and pinky finger is helpful. When the energy comes into the negative vessels, the pinky leads the arm movement. The thumb is a standard point of focus when the energy comes through the positive vessels. In this step, the energy goes down from the middle finger to meridians 1 and 2 when the joints are rotating. Step 1 requires a natural vertical dantian internal rotation so the upper chest can relax to condense the energy. Please be sure to relax the back and "dangle" the coccyx. When the hand is near the level of the dantian, energy will arrive around the ribs.

STEP 2: Moving the Dantian Horizontally; Directing Energy to the Dantian (Figs. 1c–d)
Softly shift the weight and turn the dantian to the left. Energy will come back to the dantian area due to the horizontal dantian's internal rotation. The hip's level should be parallel to the ground so the dantian has central stability.

STEP 3: Sending Energy Down to the Perineum (Figs. 1e–f)
This requires delicate instruction. Upon finishing the previous steps, the dantian begins to rotate in an oblique circle. When the hand reaches the shoulder level, the energy rises to cervical 7 (*dazhui*). In this step, the directing and governing vessels are used. Although the weight stays on the left foot, the right foot should be rooted.

STEP 4: Sending Energy to the Pinky Finger, Meridian 4 (Figs. 1g–h)
Smoothly shift the weight to the right foot and slowly turn the dantian to the right side without turning the right knee outward. After rotating the dantian, the arm should be moved afterward. If the elbow is lifted too much, the energy will not flow through the arm.

SECOND TECHNIQUE: Vertical Dantian Rotation

This second technique of dantian internal rotation is not simple to acquire; however, this small silk-reeling exercise helps one's understanding of the physical requirements and sensation of proper silk-reeling execution. Here the dantian rotates vertically, forward and backward, with the upper chest, diaphragm, and lower back. This rotation connects the force of the dantian when raising and lowering hands in practice. For example, to capitalize on properly generated energy with correct alignment while doing jumping kicks, one must use vertical dantian rotation. In this way, the energy flows through the back to the fingertips.

Preparation: Same as previous technique (Fig. 2)

STEP 1: Vertical Forward Rotation: Directing and Governing Meridians (Microcosmic Orbit) (Figs. 2a–g)

When the thumb goes outward from the dantian, energy circulates from the governing vessel to the directing vessel. This is a vertical forward rotation of the dantian, which needs close awareness to keep from hollowing the upper chest too much. The upper chest makes a natural curve during this type of dantian rotation. In this exercise, the height of the body makes downward and upward adjustments by rotating the dantian and the hands. The wrist, elbow, and shoulder joints have to make a big circle with relaxation. When the body is lowered, the energy circulates from the dantian ▸ huiyin (perineum) ▸ mingmen ▸ lingtai ▸ baihui ▸ renzhong ▸ shanzhong ▸ dantian. This is the small heavenly circle, or microcosmic orbit. You'll sense less energy in the hands as energy circulates in the microcosmic orbit.

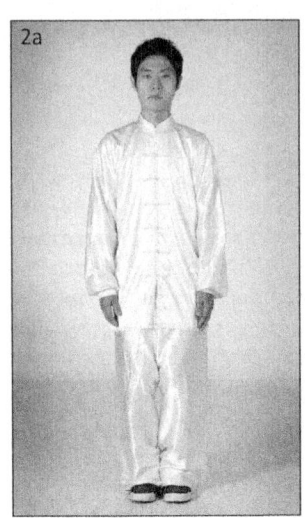

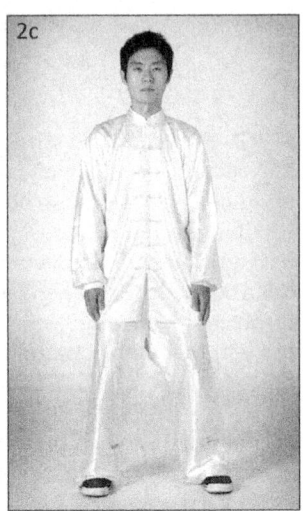

STEP 2: Reversal of Microcosmic Orbit (Figs. 2h–l)
For the vertical backward rotation of the dantian, one simply directs the thumb inward toward the dantian. With this movement, the energy circulates from the directing vessel to the governing vessel. This type of energy circulation is rare to find in Chinese medicine and qigong because it conflicts with the traditional meridians. However, Chen taijiquan masters have held this concept for a long time, basing it on a practical heritage and the principle of contradiction between yin and yang. When the thumb comes toward the dantian, the energy circulates from dantian ▸ baihun ▸ dazhui ▸ lingtai ▸ mingmen ▸ huiyin ▸ dantian. It reverses the direction of the energy flow in the small heavenly circle. With this practice, severe neck and shoulder pain can be relieved and arms will increase physical flexibility. The lungs should not be used too much in order to avoid making the shoulder tense. It is because the lower abdominals and dantian are mainly used instead of using the lungs.

THIRD TECHNIQUE: Mixed Dantian Rotation
A third type of rotation is a combination of the first and second techniques presented previously. The double-hand silk-reeling maximizes all three techniques of dantian internal rotation. It can be defined as the combination of the first type of lateral and second type of vertical rotations while practicing silk-reeling movements within the old frame forms. This mixed type of dantian internal rotation is not fixed, with unique paths throughout each movement to adhere to correct posture. To acquire this type of dantian rotation, it is crucial to be very familiar with the previous techniques. Since the classical Chen taijiquan practice forms are based on the theory of dantian rotation, their movements include many mixed dantian rotations. This concept should be kept simple, and if there is anything unclear or ambiguous about this mixed rotation, one should go back to mastering the previous exercises.

Use of the meridians becomes more complicated than in the previous exercises, since one begins to use both hands to activate the left and right sides of meridians simultaneously. However, with correct guidance and proper training of the first and second techniques, there will be no problem in applying this third technique.

Preparation: Same as previous technique (Fig. 3)

STEP 1: Simultaneously Activating Two Meridians (Fig. 3a)
If the two previous practices are properly learned, it is comfortable to activate two meridians at the same time with this third technique. As shown in the picture, the left hand activates meridian 1 while the right hand activates meridian 3. However, do not be overly concerned with trying to sense the simultaneous energy flow in these two meridians because the centralized dantian position will circulate the energy itself by a practitioner's correct movement. For example, if the dantian is centered, one will feel both feet are rooted and then the mind will become calm and peaceful. If the practitioner is not confident in using these meridians, meditating on the dantian's internal rotation would be an alternative way to acquire this exercise. Please keep the hip (*kua*) parallel to the ground. Hands and feet feel swelling or tingling if the energy is circulating correctly. If not, the whole body will become cold. Please be advised by your instructor, for that is a bad sign while doing this practice.

In this step, the weight is on the left foot and both hands are raised. Open the laogong point while relaxing the shoulders and lowering the elbows. The left knee does not go beyond the toe line, and the back has no concave or convex shape.

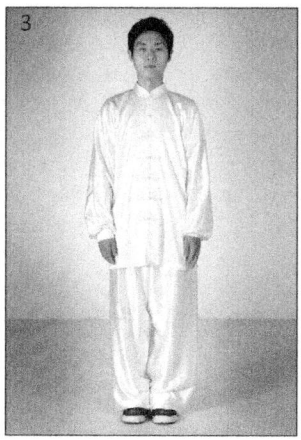

STEP 2: Rotate the Dantian Horizontally to the Right Side (Fig. 3b)
Slowly shift the weight onto the right foot with the first dantian-rotation technique, which is a horizontal rotation. The dantian leads the movement of the arms. The hips are parallel to the ground. Because meridian 2 for the left hand and meridian 4 for the right hand are being used, the dantian forms the core axis that combines these two meridians and the lower body becomes very full of energy. One's intention must stay on the dantian for the meridians to circulate energy well. If there is an error, energy will be stuck in the upper chest, and the area around the dantian will become tense. If this movement is done incorrectly, the body and hands will feel cold. This type of error should be corrected.

Step 3: Mixed Rotation of the Dantian (Figs. 3c–d)
There is no weight change, but a third technique of dantian internal rotation is being activated in this step. After the first dantian rotation is made in the previous step, the dantian makes a vertical and a horizontal rotation at the same time the energy sinks downward. Although the dantian internal rotations of the first and second techniques can be clearly felt, other dantian internal rotations can be complex and multidirectional. In this step, the yongquan meridian point feels very soft and supple due to sinking energy. Meridian 3 for the left hand and meridian 1 for the right hand are activated.

STEP 4: Horizontal Dantian Internal Rotation (Figs. 3e–h)
After the previous step, slowly change the weight to the left foot and smoothly execute a horizontal dantian internal rotation. The dantian should have a horizontal circular movement, and both hands should be around the level of dantian. If the body structure is correct, you will sense a powerful amount of energy in the governing vessel's mingmen and lingtai points. It is a common mistake for the upper body to lean, and a practitioner will not be able to sense this energy. Meridian 4 for the left hand and meridian 2 for the right hand are activated simultaneously. Using two different meridians at once is the balance and zest of yin and yang.

Double-hand silk-reeling exercises may provide some relief or cure ailments because they stimulate meridians on both sides of a practitioner's body, resulting in good energy circulation. For example, the pericardium meridian of the left arm is used while the small-intestine meridian of the right arm is activated. This method embodies Chen taijiquan's two characteristics of "using the waist as an axle" and "folding the chest and waist" while silk-reeling.

Practicing silk-reeling and forms are considered methods of energy circulation in which the dantian is the core center axis that directs all movements. The theory of dantian internal rotation is the essence of Chen taijiquan and practicing the three practical techniques as described in this article will gradually develop one's taijiquan level. As time passes, one will experience the penetration of all joints by silk-reeling energy, while physical ailments are significantly lessened by fully cultivating energy from the dantian. It is known that the particular form practiced does not matter after achieving the highest taijiquan level because the dantian controls internal energy and external motions by itself, thus allowing one's martial application to become free of form. This explains why different taijiquan styles exist.

Internal Alchemy of Chen Family Taijiquan

After a certain amount of time practicing taijiquan, one has to confirm his or her level with push-hands practices. These are hands-on exercises by two people with direct applications of the above exercises. The practice includes various exchanges of sturdiness, softness, fastness, and slowness. Chen taijiquan has five kinds of push-hands that require the third type of dantian internal rotation. In other words, push-hands practices are not helpful for those who do not have a base study of dantian internal rotation. Just practicing silk-reeling exercises is not enough to study all various changes and techniques of taijiquan. While the second routine (cannon fist) is helpful in developing explosive energy (*fajing*) with fast applications of dantian internal rotations, the first routine is able to train the dantian rotations for developing deep relaxation (*fangsong*) with slow applications of dantian internal rotations. If practicing the two characteristics of slowness and softness alone, one will not seize all the requirements of authentic taijiquan; therefore, one must express power through proper expression of explosive energy, all while employing correct dantian usage. The three types of dantian rotation are crucial for correct silk-reeling exercises and the key to understanding and practicing taijiquan forms and push-hands practice.

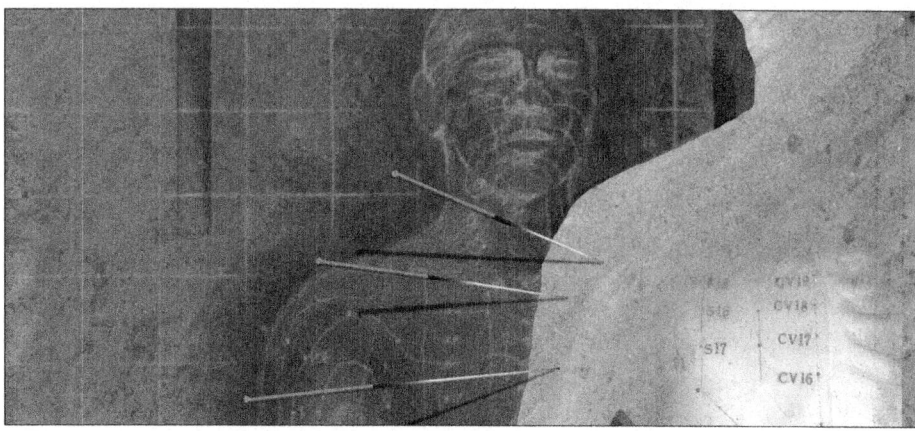

With permission from a master, a practitioner should learn the microcosmic and macrocosmic orbit techniques (small and big heavenly circle) for the internal alchemy of Chen taijiquan. If the dantian possesses powerful energy within, it should eventually circulate through the directing (*renmai*) and governing (*dumai*) meridians. This is called the microcosmic orbit, or small heavenly circle. In later stages of development, energy interpenetrates through the entire spine directly from the huiyin to the bahui point. This later level of energy interpenetration is called the macrocosmic orbit, or big heavenly circle.

As described previously, dantian breathing through the *damai* meridian is the impetus of dantian internal alchemy necessary before executing the microcosmic and macrocosmic orbits. The meridian orbits require the energy flow from the dantian to enable continued circulation. Including the direct and governing vessels, all other meridians are controlled smoothly by the full energy supplied by the dantian. By repeating correct authentic methods, one's dantian will continue to develop until the practice stops.

Historically, the three dantian internal-rotation techniques have been what the direct lineage of Chen family taijiquan masters used to develop and maintain a "golden internal alchemy." This tradition will surely continue. Please be simple and clear about these concepts, as practical application of taijiquan is not mysterious. If there is doubt or an unclear concept of taijiquan practice, it may be the case that one's instruction or understanding of this practice lacks depth. This is why authentic taijiquan lineages exist and why the techniques remain as sound in application as they were when first developed. In this day and age, taijiquan has been practiced and exists in various forms, but as a true martial practitioner, one must release form and appearance and truly contemplate the essence of taijiquan.

Chinese Glossary

chansijing	纏絲勁
chen jian zhui zhou	沈肩墜肘
Chen shi taijiquan	陳氏太極拳
chongmai	衝脈
daimai	帶脈
dantian	丹田
dantian gen	丹田根
dantian neizhuan	丹田內轉
daoyin tuna	導引吐納
dumai	督脈
fajin/fajing	發勁
han xiong ba bei	含胸拔背
jiejie guanchuan	節節貫串

Ji Xiao Xin Shu	紀效新書
pericardium meridian of the hand	手厥陰心包經
laojia yilu	老架一路
laojia erlu	老架二路
mingmen	命門
neidan	內丹
qi	氣
Qi Jiguang	戚繼光
qi jing ba mai	奇經八脈
renmai	任脈
shi er zheng jing	十二正經
ta yao	塌腰
small-intestine meridian of the hand	手太陽小腸經
spleen meridian of the foot	足太陰脾經
wei lu zhong zheng	尾閭中正
xiong yao zhe die	胸腰折疊
yang qiao mai	陽蹻脈
yang wei mai	陽維脈
yi yao wei zhou	以腰為軸
Yijing	易經
yin qiao mai	陰蹻脈
yin wei mai	陰維脈
yongquan	湧泉
zhen tou xuan	貞頭懸

Tensegrity: Development of Dynamic Balance and Internal Power in Taijiquan

by Michael Rosario Graycar and Rachel Tomlinson, M.Ed.

Photographs by Michael Rosario Graycar & Ryan Craig.

The internal martial art of Chen-style taijiquan has been increasing in prominence throughout the United States and the world. Over the years many practitioners have worked with high-level masters, but few have developed the skills demonstrated by these masters. Many of these masters do not possess the English-language skills to impart the "internal feeling" of their given art onto their students. Here's where many Western practitioners run into the biggest issue: rote learning through imitation will not lead to mastery. Only by having a clear understanding of the language of the "internal feeling" of taijiquan can any headway be made.

Languages to Develop "Internal Feeling"

According to Grandmaster Chen Xiaowang (Berwick & Butler, 2003: 36), three languages are necessary to understand taiji:

1) The language of speaking and writing: to explain and theorize
2) The language of the body: to demonstrate and see
3) The language of corrections: to feel (the most important language)

The masters are able to use languages 2 and 3 cited above. However, the English language of speaking and writing has often been deficient in enabling these masters to describe and impart the "internal feeling" of taijiquan to their students.

Therefore, some masters and practitioners have used inappropriate scientific models to describe the static and movement mechanics of the body. Namely, the body has been compared to buildings in which the skeleton is stacked in a compressive state, like a column structure. Modern science tells us that this model is not correct. If bones met other bones under compression, the bones and joints would quickly deteriorate.

The other model used in describing the static body mechanics in taijiquan is the arch, where the tailbone and pelvis act like a keystone. Obviously, the basic mechanics appear to make sense when two feet are on the ground; however, as Grandmaster Chen regularly demonstrates, the ability to root on one foot would not be possible under the arch analogy.

The problem with both of these analogies is that compressive structures can only deal with load force acting directly on them following the pull of gravity. Any shear or torque forces acting on a building structure quickly undermine its structural integrity, and can cause the structure to be unstable. Through demonstrations of internal masters, this is simply not the case. These masters can receive both shear and torque forces while maintaining structural integrity.

At the same time, the definition of movement mechanics has also been flawed. Viewing movement like a levering system does not take into account the forces involved in performing the simplest actions, such as picking up a watermelon. As Dr. Stephen Levin notes, "Calculating loads with the body as a lever-beam, linear Newtonian model will create forces that rip muscle, crush bone and exhaust energy" (2002: 375).

We can see from the present paradigm why the human body may be suffering from degenerative diseases, such as carpal tunnel, tendonitis, arthritis, and myofascial disorders, among others. When we treat the body like a stacked column, compressing the structure with the pull of gravity and using our joints in a fixed lever-type manner, we put undue wear and tear on the body as a whole.

So, what model based on science can describe the body mechanics truly experienced in taijiquan and other internal martial arts?

Tensegrity, or tensional integrity, as defined by *Wikipedia*, is "a property of structures with an integrity based on a balance between tension and compression components." Furthermore, "within the structure, the compression-bearing rigid struts stretch, or tense, the flexible, tension-bearing members, while those tension-bearing members compress the rigid struts. These counteracting forces, which equilibrate throughout the structure, are what enable it to stabilize itself" (Ingber, 1998: 49). So, a structure formed under the principles of tensegrity is under a state of pre-stress even before an external force can be applied.

This scientific model can be applied to both the static and movement mechanics of the human body. According to Dr. Donald Ingber, "in other words, in the complex tensegrity structure inside every one of us, bones are the compression struts, and muscles, tendons and ligaments are the tension-bearing members" (1998: 50).

This type of structure is stable through the constant interplay of its tension (*yang*) and compressive (*yin*) parts. This prestress (*wuji*, "without ridgepole") balances the body regardless of its shape or orientation. The practitioner has the ability to stand on one or both legs, or on the hands, while still maintaining whole-body equilibrium. The body is no longer bound to stacking or bracing the force into the ground; it can move freely while dissipating any force that acts on it throughout the entire structure such that each part takes up a fraction of the force.

One of the interesting qualities of tensegrity is its ability to shape change, particularly when the structure is made of both flexible-tensile material and compressive-rigid structural parts, as seen in Figure 1. A tensegrity object can expand or compact, or turn and move, in relationship to forces acting upon it without becoming slack or pulled apart. As soon as a force acts on it, all parts adjust to maintain the integrity of the structure. When the force is released, the structure springs back to its original shape. The faster the external force compacts the structure, the faster it springs back, unleashing its stored force (*fajing*: "explosive power discharge").

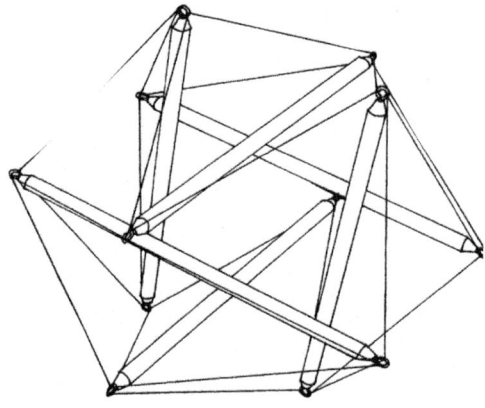

Figure 1

Consequently, the only way to destroy a tensegrity structure is to know the inherent weakness in the materials in the structure and exploit that weakness. For example, in a structure comprised of wood and rubber bands, fire or a saw could quickly destroy the structure. And while overextension would eventually rip the rubber bands, any compacting force would not destroy the structure. In theory, we physically start with our body parts as strong as wood and rubber bands, and transform them into hardened steel beams and flexible steel cables.

Using the above tensegrity model, we can interpret and possibly understand the archaic language of the taiji classics. We will use three stanzas from the classics and the foundation-training exercises of Chen taijiquan to further discuss this model and develop a clear language to describe and understand the "internal feeling."

According to the taiji classics, "Stand like a balanced scale, (move) lively like a cartwheel" (Yang, 1991: 220).

Under tensegrity principles and mechanics, the body can "stand like a balanced scale," whether it is on one foot or two, since the fundamental principle of tensegrity is that the compressive and tension elements balance out, creating a sense of wuji in the body.

Although this analogy uses the term cartwheel, this type of wheel is a rigid structure, under constant compression. When a cartwheel is in motion, only the spokes in line with the pull of gravity are sustaining loads at any one time.

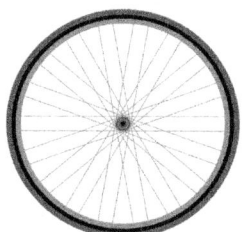

Figure 2

A bicycle wheel with wire spokes (Figure 2), on the other hand, is an example of a tensegrity structure. The forces are divided evenly across all of the spokes and the compression of the rim, while the hub floats in the tension network of the spokes, allowing it to turn freely under the load force acting around it. So, using the bicycle wheel instead of the cartwheel, the *dantian* ("cinnabar or red field"; body center) is the hub with the ability to freely turn, while the limbs act as the rim and the soft tissue connecting them to the dantian acts like the spokes. When any outside forces act on the limbs, the compressive aspect of the limbs themselves and the tensional aspect of the soft tissue connecting the limbs through the torso to the dantian zeros out the force so that the dantian is not inhibited from freely rotating.

The cartwheel is really the analogy of our present, untrained state. Before intensive internal training, we tend to lack tensegrity, so that any force acting on our body instantly invades our dantian center, stutters it, and destroys our centralized equilibrium. It will then force us to overtly tense localized areas of the body to maintain upright balance, which creates the column or stacked structure.

To develop tensegrity, we need to understand that it works from the cellular level, to the tissue level, to the whole body structure. "Thus, from the molecules to the bones and muscles and tendons of the human body, tensegrity is clearly nature's preferred building system. Only tensegrity, for example, can explain how every time you move your arm, your skin stretches, your extracellular matrix extends, your cells distort, and the interconnected molecules that form the internal framework of the cell feel the pull-all without any breakage or discontinuity" (Ingber, 1998: 56).

Fundamental Taijiquan Practices to Enhance Tensegrity Mechanics

In Chen taijiquan the fundamental methods of developing these principles are harnessed through the practice of post standing (*zhanzhuang*) and silk-reeling exercises (*chansigong*). These methods enable the practitioner to develop both static and movement tensegrity mechanics.

Through post standing practice with direct corrections by a master, the practitioner can develop the feeling of a tensegrity body structure in which all parts are neither too tense nor too relaxed, producing the central equilibrium state. The overall goal of standing is to produce natural and effortless action (*wu wei*).

When the practitioner begins standing, many aspects of the body are out of alignment with the pull of gravity. This causes excess localized tension in parts of the body. This can be seen in Figure 3a. The shoulders, hips, and ankles are not in alignment. The shoulders and chest are lifted, causing excess stress in the upper torso. The diagonal line on the body shows the body mass lifting forward, up, and away from the pull of gravity. The line at the lower back demonstrates the excessive curvature of the lumbar spine, causing the dantian to shift out and forward, which lifts the hips and tailbone up and back, decreasing the angle between lumbar and tailbone. The upper line illustrates the forward curvature of the neck, lifting the jaw and head up and out. As a result of these unbalanced forces, any external force acting directly on the torso would cause the structure to be rendered unstable.

In Figure 3b, Master Ren Guangyi corrects Michael's alignment, bringing his body into a state of equilibrium.

In Figure 3c, Michael demonstrates a balanced state. His shoulders, hips, and ankles form a line. The dantian creates an equalized force from front to back and top to bottom, which causes the angle from the tailbone to the lower back to increase, releasing the localized tension in the lumbar region. With the neck and the lower back opening up and the jaw and chest relaxing down, the body balances out all of the opposing forces, which exhibits the principles of tensegrity.

The ability to sense these changes in the body's structure from unstable to a balanced tensegrity structure relates to the body's proprioceptive sense. According to www.bio-medicine.com, "proprioception" (from Latin *proprius*, meaning "one's own") is the sense of the position of parts of the body, relative to other neighboring parts of the body."

What Does the Proprioceptive Sense Mean within Our Taijiquan Practice?

This sense of the body is partially responsible for how the body creates an unconscious balanced state. Therefore, this sense helps to develop a habit that's hard to break, since it causes a feeling of comfort in how the body relates to its environment. Post-standing practice can be an intensely painful experience for the beginner. By causing a complete structural change, muscles are stressed in different ways than the normal state of the body. The more we resist the pain, the harder it will be for the body to recalibrate the proprioceptive sense to the more efficiently balanced state.

When our body experiences intense pain, we tend to internally run away from the corrections and unconsciously seek out our old ways of standing and holding our body. On the other hand, if we grit our teeth and force ourselves to hold the posture, we end up developing excessive strength tensions, which again negates our body's tensegrity. Therefore, we need to reprogram our motor movements so that we can maintain a balance of tension and compression throughout the body.

Only by driving oneself consistently and developing the practice into a meditation so that the mental and physical state can become comfortable and relaxed will the proprioceptive sense change to the new demands. By connecting a deep sense of respiration causing micromovements to occur in the lumbar spine, the practice of this helps bring the practitioner's consciousness into this meditative state.

Once the proprioceptive sense has been reprogrammed, the biggest obstacle has been overcome and the wuji stance has become our unconscious balanced state. Unlike many other martial arts where the taking of a balanced stance is a conscious effort, in taijiquan, wuji is the natural state of the body. Hence, our bodies are always ready to act and react to any external force.

The practitioner can further develop wuji and extend the tensegrity state of the body's structure by holding various postures from the taijiquan forms. In Figure 4, Master Ren demonstrates the entrance into the "White Crane" posture from new frame first routine (*xinjia yilu*). When the hip is sunk and the knee-to-foot line is perpendicular, the body appears to be unstable due to the mass of the torso being sunken behind the feet. The location of his center of gravity in relationship to the ground is marked with an X.

white crane

In the stacking method, without a chair—or a tail—it is virtually impossible to lower the body behind the feet and maintain balance on all sides. The structure should only be stable and strong from right to left, where either foot can act as the support to offset the pressure. Any force forward or backward should destroy the structure, and send him on his back or chest, respectively.

For the average practitioner, the knees typically pass over the toes and the heels start to rise off the floor, creating a stacked structure and putting excessive load force on the knees and ankles in an angle that cannot be supported with balanced integrity.

However, in reality, the tensegrity of Master Ren's structure allows for him to maintain a relaxed, balanced state with no excessive forces building at the knee and ankle. The quadriceps and hamstrings both work together like tension steel cables to balance out the load forces, while his femurs, shins, and hips create the compressive stability of his structure with every other part of his body acting in concert.

Mastering Wuji

The taiji classics state, "First look to expanding, then look to compacting, then you approach perfection" (Yang, 1991: 227).

The above statement can be very misleading. In a literal tone, we could say to stretch out your moves as far as you can, and then make them tight—and you're a master. We all know that it's not this simple.

If we return to the tensegrity model, we can see the truth in this statement. The larger the structure, the more stable it will be, due to the amount of prestress internally acting on it. When it is compacted by an external force, the body will store the force within the structure. In effect, the force is being concentrated as the structure is compacted. Consequently, when the force is suddenly released and the structure is able to resume its original shape, it does so with an explosive release of force in three-dimensional space.

In Chen-style taijiquan, we call this aspect of the curriculum "large frame training." After we learn to expand within the structure of basic wuji standing and the form postures, we begin to increase the range of motion of the joints and space within the joints, which in turn increases the synovial fluids in the joints, as well as the fluids in the spine, sacrum, hips, the whole abdominal region, and the fascia lining of the entire body.

As we all know, humans are comprised mostly of water. The fascia serves as a flexible membrane that forms intricate layers, similar to plastic wrap, which holds the water. These layers of connective tissue hold us together; the tissue is the most abundant component that makes up the human body. Due to the compressive element of the fascia, it maintains a constant pressure in the body, known as hydrostatic pressure (*peng jin*, "ward off/universal inflation force"). We see this in the plant world as well: since a plant has no skeleton, it is the work of hydrostatic pressure (*peng*) that makes it stand up.

Masters regularly tell us that we need to develop this *peng* energy. Through the tensegrity model, we now have a systematic method from which to develop this elusive energy. Now we can see why typical practitioners cannot replicate the feats of high-level masters, such as bouncing the opponent away on first contact. They do not have enough hydrostatic pressure and cannot maintain the tensegrity of their structures.

Through the changing of our somatic balance state, from stacking to tensegrity, we start to increase the fluids in the body. Since a tensegrity structure always moves with the force direction, the structure provides the mechanical advantage of automatically having the ability to balance out any force the opponent tries to apply to our body. With the structure maintaining the integrity of the body center (*dantian*) to react, the body can efficiently balance or compact the force without creating direct resistance.

After the practitioner is able to develop and maintain tensegrity while the structure is static (*wuji* state), the quest is to effectively compact and expand the body in a balanced state through rotation and movement. Silk reeling is the primary method for developing this ability.

Circles, Spirals, and Folding: The Way Tensegrity Moves

As stated in the taiji classics, "Once in motion, everything in motion. Once at rest, everything at rest. Tugged into motion, back and forth. The breath-energy [qi] adheres to the back, and is absorbed into the spine" (Wells, 2005: 237).

Tensegrity theory teaches us that once an external force is applied to the structure, the entire structure simultaneously changes its shape. There is no sequential linking, like a domino effect; rather all parts change and reorient to the force to maintain the structure. Obviously, when the structure is put in motion, every part moves. Once the force stops, the structure stops and returns to its normal prestress state (*wuji*).

Again, the tensegrity theory proves the above line from the taiji classics. When the tensegrity body is tugged or pressed, everything goes into motion through expansion and contraction, hidden within movement and rotation.

With regard to the last stanza of this quote, we are not here to prove or disprove the existence of bioenergy (*qi*). If we look at the life energy as related to respiration and our hydrostatic state, we can see some truth in this statement. By suspending the spine, utilizing the theory of the tensegrity truss, such as the Kurilpa Bridge in Brisbane, Australia, we can effectively create this expanded tensile shape with the spine serving as the powerful connector between the body's center (*dantian*) and the rest of the body. Just as the Kurilpa Bridge works, the spine can move force in either direction while maintaining its own centralized balance, even though the spinal shape will subtly change in relationship to the stress forces.

Now the body has a pathway to move our own force and our opponents force without any part developing any localized resistance or excessive tension. When hydrostatic pressure (spinal fluid) increases in the spine, it creates suspension between the vertebrae, maintaining the compressive aspects of each vertebra within itself while the intervertebral discs serve as the tensional parts.

If post standing is a method to develop static tensegrity, silk-reeling is a method to develop movement tensegrity. The parts of the body expand and contract in coordination with the movement of the spine, as described above. Silk-reeling provides a repetitive pattern of body movements that, when developed with a calm and controlled mind, can further develop the proprioceptive sense. If this pattern is forced, it is not yet the natural state of the body, and the correct "internal feelings" will never be realized.

In the following illustrations, Master Ren depicts the four main points of the silk-reeling movements, as taught by Grandmaster Chen Xiaowang. This slow, focused, repetitive pattern training provides the setting for the practitioner to allow the proprioceptive information to be sent to the brain, which will stimulate an intense dynamic and internal awareness to further enhance the mind/body integration.

Numerous authors have written on the fundamentals of silk-reeling; consequently, we will only provide a brief outline, along with a description of the "internal feeling" of the movements, which is the most important.

The silk-reeling being demonstrated by Master Ren is considered the one-handed positive circle silk-reeling movement. He is demonstrating the left side only. This movement can also be done with the right hand, or with both hands coordinating together or alternating the pattern.

Grandmaster Chen teaches four important energy qualities within the silk-reeling pattern:

1) qi descending to the waist
2) qi gathering at dantian center
3) qi filling the back
4) qi filling out to the fingertips

These four energy qualities are the root of silk-reeling. Just shifting the weight and tracing the circle in the air with the arm will not develop anything but stamina and muscle tone. Without the correct "internal feeling" developed within silk reeling, the exercise is practically useless.

Master Ren demonstrates these energies of silk-reeling. Through the reeling movement, the qi travels through the entire system, unobstructed. Starting with energy in the hand (Figure 5a), Master Ren is at a stable point to start moving the qi from the extremities toward the waist.

In Figure 5b, Master Ren demonstrates "qi descending to the waist." The correct feeling under tensegrity rules will be a uniform compacting of the structure, three dimensionally, from the fingertips inward toward the torso. At this point there is no weight shift, and the body is still resting mainly on the left leg.

In Figure 5c, we see Master Ren has now shifted his weight to the right and has reached his limit of the compacting side of the equation. Here he has achieved "qi gathering at dantian center." Now the left side of the body, through the compacting from outside to in and left to right, has prepared a path for an external force to follow without resistance.

In Figure 5d, his weight is focused on the right foot while the torso has rotated, effectively releasing a load stress that would be acting on his left side if an opponent were there. As we know from tensegrity theory, once a force isn't directly acting on it, the structure seeks to move from a compacted state to an expanded state. Here, we have "qi filling the back" with the feeling of a slow, steady expansion through the left side of the back up through the shoulder.

As Master Ren completes the reeling cycle, he expands and extends into the "qi filling out to the fingertips" position in Figure 5e. The weight has shifted back to the left foot from the slow, steady expansion from the back shoulder area to the fingertips. The feeling of a three-dimensional expansion on the left side of the body includes both the left side of the back and chest/ribcage area as well as the entire left arm expanding uniformly out to the palm and fingertips.

The cycle returns to Figure 5b in a continuous, repetitive pattern.

The Need for Fangsong to Fajing

For anyone who trains with any of the Chen taijiquan masters, a commonly repeated term is *fangsong*. This term is commonly translated as "relaxation." Nevertheless, Grandmaster Chen Zhenglei describes fangsong within taijiquan as a relaxed, extended, expanded, pliable, stable structure, which is another way to describe tensegrity in certain states. As we see from the above information, relaxation is only one component of fangsong. In tensegrity structures, through the constant state of tension/compression on the microscale, you will observe the subtle "relaxing" of some tensional components as others increase strength to maintain a balanced state under any pressure. The tensegrity theory offers a mechanical understanding of how the body and mind can achieve this fangsong state, both physically and mentally.

When we can develop this fangsong state, all the requirements to explosively release a tremendous amount of force on our opponent are realized, and Chen taijiquan "explosive power discharge" (*fajing*), with its apparently relaxed, effortless expression, can impact the opponent without a loss of our tensegrity. In figure 6a, the opponent's force enables Master Ren to compact into the center of his structure. In figure 6b, once the opponent's force is released off of the center, Master Ren explosively expands from his center through his opponent, which violently launches his opponent off the ground without a loss of his structural integrity.

Tensegrity: Defining a New View of Body Maintenance and Development

The tensegrity model and the biology of hydrostatic pressure provide the language to describe both static and movement mechanics in the human body, particularly relating to Chen taijiquan and internal martial arts practice. The connective tissue, bones, and spine work in coordination to provide a stable structure from the inside out for the body. We can apply these ideas into almost every facet of internal martial arts curricula, as well as anything that we do in life.

When applied to the martial arts, the tremendous power exhibited by high-level practitioners is fully explainable. On the internal side, you have the compacting and concentrating of power and relaxed, explosive, expansive release, combined with the external power of speed and mass in motion.

When we look toward the healing side of internal martial arts, we can see why these arts can be enjoyed by the elderly and injured, and provide the environment for sometimes seemingly miraculous healings to occur. Since the body is being reprogrammed to move with the least amount of resistance and expenditure of energy, it now has the energy to do what it is intended to do: maintain itself.

Furthermore, some orthopedic doctors, chiropractors, and bodywork practitioners have started using tensegrity as a basis of their practice. Therefore, the implications for body development and enhancement are far reaching, particularly in terms of repetitive strain injuries and personal physical growth.

Taiji Applications:
Tensegrity in Motion

According to Dr. Donald Ingber, "A local force can change the shape of an entire tensegrity structure," while maintaining the integrity of the entire structure. In applications, the taiji practitioner employs wuji to maintain the tensegrity structure. Then the opponent's forces can be compacted or expanded while the practitioner utilizes postural fluid shape changing through folding and turning actions to maintain his or her own balanced state such that no localized resistance or excessive tension is experienced throughout the movement.

The following series of applications will demonstrate a few possible ways the body can maintain tensegrity while under resistive pressure from an attacker and effectively maintain a relaxed, fluid body action, utilizing silk reeling and folding methods.

Protect the Heart
1. The attacker (on left) is violently pushing both of the defender's arms down at the elbows. This causes the defender's body to compact toward the center, with the weight on the left foot.
2. The defender splits the forces by raising his right fist straight up and lowering his left fist.
3. The defender folds both of his fists/arms over the attacker's arms, towards his own center. This brings him into a fully compacted state.
4. From this compacting, the defender starts explosively expanding his structure, and extends his fists, with the right fist higher than the left, into his attacker's chest. The fists end level with his heart region, while his body relaxes back into the wuji position.

Single Whip
1. When the attacker attempts to lock his right arm, the defender maintains his compacted, balanced state (*wuji*).
2. The defender then folds his right elbow, raising it above his attacker's arm while preparing to sink down on his right leg.
3. The defender continues to fold his elbow/arm on top of his attacker's arm, sinking his weight down on his right leg. At the same time, he uses his left hand to grab his attacker's wrist.
4. The defender continues to grab, torque, and lock his attacker's right wrist to control him. As his body explosively rises, he uses his right hook hand to strike at the attacker's head, which naturally returns the defender to a balanced wuji position.

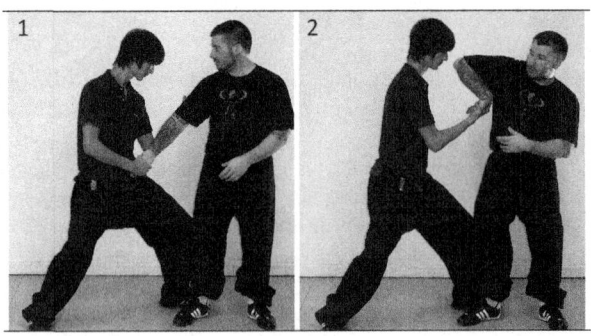

Six Sealing, Four Closing

1. When the attacker attempts to suddenly pull down then upward on the defender's right arm, he maintains his compacted, balanced stance.
2. The defender transfers his weight to the left side and lifts his right leg. At the same time, utilizing "ward off" (*peng*), his right hand lifts his attacker's right arm, as he grabs the attacker's left wrist with his left hand.
3. The defender steps behind the attacker with his right foot, keeping his weight on the left side, and proceeds to fold and twist both of the attacker's arms toward his left side, while the defender's body rotates and diverts the attacker's power away from his center as he coils into his left leg.
4. The defender starts to explosively unwind and expand his structure as he transfers his weight right. His body then descends onto his right leg as he strikes both hands toward his attacker's center. The defender's attack ends with his hands at a 45-degree angle from his center, while his weight is relaxing down on his right foot, returning his body to its natural wuji state.

GLOSSARY

- 纏絲功 *chansigong*: silk-reeling exercises
- 丹田 *dantian*: "elixir field" or physical center of gravity, located in the abdomen
- 發勁 *fajing*: explosive power discharge
- 放松 *fang-song*: relaxation; or, a relaxed, extended, expanded, pliable state
- 掤勁 *peng jin*: "ward off/universal inflation force"
- 氣 *qi*: bioenergy
- 無極 *wuji*: without ultimate; ultimateless
- 站樁 *zhanzhuang* : standing like a post; or, a method of training in many Chinese martial arts in which static postures are used for physical training, to develop efficiency of movement, perfection of structural alignment, and hence maximal strength, for martial applications
- proprioception: the sense of the position of parts of the body, relative to other neighboring parts of the body
- tensegrity: a property of structures with an integrity based on a balance between tension and compression components

Acknowledgment

A special thanks goes to Master Ren Guangyi for his high standard of teaching, support, and collaborating on this article. Also, thanks to Ryan Craig and Aaron Ocker for being great attackers.

Bibliography

Berwick, S. and Butler, D. (2003). Comments on selections from Chen Xin's *Illustrated Explanations of Chen taijiquan*. *Journal of Asian Martial Arts*, 12(4): 34–47.

Ingber, D. (1998). The architecture of life. *Scientific American*, 278(1): 48–57.

Levin, S. (2002). The tensegrity-truss as a model for spine mechanics: Biotensegrity. *Journal of Mechanics in Medicine and Biology*, 2(3–4), 375–388.

Proprioception. (n.d.). Retrieved February 13, 2010, from Bio-Medicine.org website: http://www.bio-medicine.org/biology-definition/Proprioception/.

Tensegrity. (2010). In *Wikipedia*. Retrieved February 13, 2010, from http://en.wikipedia.org/wiki/Tensegrity#Basic_Tensegrity_structures.

Wells, M. (2005). *Scholar boxer: Chang Naizhou's theory of internal martial arts and the evolution of taijiquan*. Berkeley, CA: North Atlantic Books.

Yang, J. (1991). *Advanced Yang style tai chi chuan: Volume one: Tai chi theory and tai chi jing*. Jamaica Plains, MA: YMAA Publication Center.

index

baihui acupoint, 49, 72, 82
Book of Changes (*Yijing*), 45–46
Cannon Fist (paochui), 4, 33, 37, 39, 46, 69, 87
Chen Bing, 73
Chen Changxing, 34, 36
Chen Fake, 6, 35
Chen Qingping, 35
Chen Yu, 73
Chen Village (Chenjiagou), 2, 6, 32–35, 49
Chen Wangting, 36, 38–41, 46, 69–70
Chen Xiaowang, 6, 12, 33–38, 43, 45, 59, 73, 90, 98
Chen Xiaoxing, 73
Chen Zhaokui, 5–6, 12
Chen Zhenglei, 100
damai meridian, 77–78, 88
dantian, 15, 38–39, 45, 47–57, 63, 67, 69–70, 72–74, 76–88, 93–94, 97–99
dumai meridian, 88
eight methods/energies (bafa), 37, 49
explosive energy (fajing), 37, 41, 43–44, 46, 48, 69, 87, 92, 100
extraordinary meridians, 70–74, 76
fangsong, 79, 87, 100
Feng Zhiqiang, 1–2, 6–7, 12, 17–19, 21
first routine (yilu), 34–37, 43, 46, 95
Fu Zhongwen, 6
Gu Liuxin, 6, 12
Hong Junsheng, 6
horizontal dantian rotation, 73, 79, 85–86
huiyin acupoint, 49, 71–72, 76, 82–83, 88
Hunyuan Gong, 17
laogong, 75–76, 84
locking techniques (qinna), 2–3, 13, 20–21, 26–32, 36–37, 40, 58–59, 63, 68
Ma Yueliang, 6

mingmen acupoint, 48, 71–73, 76–78, 82–83, 86
new frame (xinjia), 35, 37–38, 95
old frame (laojia), 34–35, 37–38, 69–70, 84
proprioception, 95
push-hands (tuishou), 2–5, 10, 12–17, 19–21, 36–37, 40, 46–47, 58–59, 87
Qi Jiquang, 33, 70
qigong, 2, 7, 9, 13–17, 19–20, 31, 35, 38, 40, 42, 83
Ren Guangyi, 32, 34–35, 38–40, 44, 47, 58, 94
renmai meridian, 88
second routine (erlu), 3–4, 17–18, 36–37, 39, 46, 69, 87
Shaolin Temple, 2, 33
silk-reeling (changsijing, chansigong), 2, 13–17, 19–25, 31, 35, 37, 40, 42–43, 46–49, 52, 54, 57–59, 70–74, 76, 78–87, 94, 98–99
standard meridians, 71, 73–74, 76
standing post (zhanzhuang), 14, 17, 35, 39–40, 42–43, 45–47, 49, 52, 58–59, 71–72, 77–79, 94
Su Jianyun, 6
Su Lutang, 35
Tang Hao, 32
tensegrity, 90–91, 97
vertical dantian rotation, 78–79, 81–85
Wang Peisheng, 6
wuji, 4, 45–46, 52, 92–93, 95, 97, 101–103
Wu Jianquan, 34
Wu Xiubao, 2
Yang Chengfu, 34
Yang Luchan, 34–35
Yang Zhengduo, 6
Yuan Shiming, 2–3
Yao Hanchen, 35
yongquan acupoint, 49, 85
Zhang Xitang, 2, 6

Printed in Great Britain
by Amazon